A LIBERATION ALBUM

Vehicles driven by soldiers of the 1st Canadian Corps were swamped with civilians when the troops liberated Utrecht on 7 May 1945.

A LIBERATION ALBUM

Canadians in the Netherlands 1944-45

Edited by David Kaufman

Historical text by Michiel Horn

Based on the film "Liberation!"
produced and directed by John Muller

McGraw-Hill Ryerson Limited
Toronto / Montreal / New York

A Liberation Album: Canadians in the Netherlands 1944-45

ISBN 0-07-092429-5

1 2 3 4 5 6 7 8 9 10 BP 9 8 7 6 5 4 3 2 1 0

Printed and bound in Canada by The Bryant Press Limited

The excerpt from *Fun Tomorrow* by John Morgan Gray is reprinted by permission of Macmillan of Canada.

Maps drawn by David Hunter. The maps in Chapters 1, 2 and 3 are adapted from C.P. Stacey's *The Victory Campaign* in The Official History of the Canadian Army in the Second World War, Vol. III (Ottawa: The Queen's Printer, 1966).

Canadian Cataloguing in Publication Data

Main entry under title:
A Liberation album

Based on the film "Liberation!" produced and directed by John Muller.
Bibliography: p.
Includes index.
ISBN 0-07-092429-5

1. World War, 1939-1945 — Personal narratives, Dutch.
2. Netherlands — History — German occupation, 1940-1945.
3. Canadians in the Netherlands. I. Kaufman, David, date II. Horn, Michiel date   III. Liberation!
(Motion picture)
D802.N47L52   940.54′81′492   C80-094705-3

Contents

Preface

The idea for this book originated with John Muller, a young Dutch filmmaker who settled recently in Canada with his family. He wanted to create a film project that would demonstrate a connection between his former country of residence and his new home; he found his subject in the story of the liberation of the Netherlands by the First Canadian Army in the last year of the Second World War. As a new immigrant, John Muller was acutely aware of the lack of positive national images in Canadian history as it is popularly understood, and he felt that a film about the liberation of the Netherlands would be a fitting and strong counterpoint to the numerous accounts of the Canadian misadventure at Dieppe in 1942.

In addition to planning his film production, John Muller also took steps to have a book produced based on the same subject matter. He asked me to edit the volume, and brought me together with Michiel Horn, a Dutch-born professor of history at Glendon College of York University in Toronto. From the beginning of our association, Michiel Horn and I agreed that this book was not intended to be the definitive account of a certain episode in Canadian military history; we decided, rather, to focus on the human elements in the story. Michiel Horn wrote the historical text with a view towards placing the liberation in its social as well as military and political contexts, and I adapted material from John Muller's film and conducted many new interviews in order to illuminate the events of the liberation with personal recollections. When these textual elements were placed in juxtaposition with the photographic resources at our disposal it became clear that we had produced what the Dutch call a *gedenkboek*, or what may be termed in English, a commemorative album.

The production of this book would not have been possible without the existence of a wonderful photographic resource, the Department of National Defence collection which is now deposited in the photographic section of the Public Archives of Canada. The D.N.D. photographs of World War II are superb on a technical level; all the photographs were taken with medium format cameras and many of the negatives possess excellent characteristics of tone and sharpness. In addition, the thousands of negatives in the collection are cleary numbered and captioned and consequently are easy to work with and identify.

From the historical point of view, the collection is not strongest in its depiction of actual combat, the apparent reason for this being that Canadian army photographers were neither encouraged nor permitted to work at the front lines during most periods of fighting. However, the army photographers were always close to the front lines, and when combat conditions allowed, they were able to move about freely and capture on film a wider range of human activities and situations. In the Netherlands in particular there was constant interaction of a strong emotional tenor between the soldiers and the civilians, and it is here that the photographic record proved to be especially moving, and therefore, most valuable for this book.

I would like to thank John Muller for urging me to participate in this project, and Michiel Horn, for agreeing to give up most of his spare time to write his part of the volume. I am grateful to the staff of the photographic section of the Public Archives of Canada for all their assistance and their prompt service in providing photographic prints. I would like to thank Drs. Henrik Henrichs who located valuable archive materials in the Netherlands. I owe a large debt of gratitude to all the people who permitted me (and in a few cases, Michiel) to intrude upon their lives and interview them about subjects and events that were, to some extent, painful to recall; not all these interviews could be published but I thank equally all those who agreed to speak to us. Finally, I would like to mention Robin Brass, of McGraw-Hill Ryerson, who encouraged Michiel Horn and me to write this book notwithstanding its unorthodox structure and the short period of time available for its production.

DAVID KAUFMAN

When John Muller approached me early in 1979 to write the historical text of a commemorative album on the liberation of the Netherlands the time was propitious. In 1976 I had commenced research on the Canadian Army in the Netherlands, but my progress had been halted by the fact that the Army Papers in the Public Archives of Canada were a closed collection. I am very grateful to Philip Chaplin of the Armed Forces Historical Directorate for his work in examining and clearing the many volumes I had asked to see. They were available to me just in time to do the research that was crucial to my contribution to this book. I wish to thank, too, those staff members who helped me at the Public Archives of Canada, the Royal Canadian Military Institute in Toronto, the State Institute for War Documentation in Amsterdam, and several municipal archives in the Netherlands.

MICHIEL HORN

Introduction

"We had to wait a few days until the Canadians arrived. Every day we went out with a basket of lilacs. I wore my father's shoes."

"I remember standing there, looking down the road which they would use to enter The Hague. On the third day, I saw a tank in the distance, with one soldier's head above it, and the blood drained out of my body, and I thought: *Here comes liberation*. And as the tank came nearer and nearer, I had no breath left, and the soldier stood up, and he was like a saint. There was a big hush over all the people, and it was suddenly broken by a big scream, as if it was out of the earth. And the people climbed on the tank, and took the soldier out, and they were crying. And we were running with the tanks and the jeeps, all the way into the city."

Two sisters, then in their late teens, recall May 8, 1945, when units of the 1st Canadian Infantry Division moved into The Hague. On that same day the Canadians also entered the other towns and cities of "Fortress Holland," the western part of the Netherlands. No one who witnessed that day is likely ever to forget it. The Dutch are not on the whole a demonstrative people, but on that day they were beyond themselves. They laughed and wept and danced, they waved their red, white and blue flags and orange banners, they screamed themselves hoarse, they jumped on and into tanks, trucks, jeeps and halftracks, embracing Canadian soldiers as if they were old friends returned from a long and hazardous journey. Thus they celebrated their release from Nazi oppression.

The Dutch threw themselves into this frenzied celebration in spite of fatigue and hunger. In the winter months just past they had stared death in the face, death by starvation or by inundation of their land. Many Netherlanders did not survive the five years of war and German occupation. But now the war was over, and the presence of the Canadians was proof that they were free. And the normally restrained Netherlanders went almost insane from the joy of it.

In May of 1980 special celebrations took place in Amsterdam, Nijmegen and other Dutch cities. May 5, the day that the German forces in the western and central Netherlands capitulated, has since 1945 been a day of thanksgiving, and more than once Canadians have been asked to participate in its celebration. This year a special effort was made. Several organizations worked from 1979 on to identify members of the First Canadian Army which swept so triumphantly into the north and west in the spring of 1945. (The south had been freed the previous autumn by American, British, Canadian and Polish troops.) Hundreds of Canadian veterans travelled to the Netherlands to help celebrate the 35th anniversary of the Liberation, and to pay tribute to the memory of their comrades who died in the effort to free the Dutch people.

These celebrations are evidence of the continuing warm relationship between Canada and the Netherlands. The links between the two countries, forged in the heat of battle and its aftermath, were strengthened further after the war when thousands of Dutch emigrants headed for Canada, numbering more than 160,000 by 1960, and almost 200,000 ten years later. Through all these years the debt of gratitude has not been forgotten; Holland still thanks Canada, and many citizens of both countries remember vividly the events of 35 years ago. In this spirit of remembrance and celebration, this album of words and pictures is published. Not only does it mark the anniversary of the Dutch regaining their freedom, but it also commemorates a singular and noble Canadian achievement.

THE LOW COUNTRIES

Prologue

The Capitulation of the Netherlands

On that morning of May 10, 1940, I was awakened at about 4 a.m. by what seemed to be a thunderstorm. After listening for a few moments, I realized that it was not thunder but shooting; so I leaned out of the window to see what was going on. All around people were hanging out of windows and somebody said something about German planes. I went downstairs and turned on the radio and there it was affirmed. The announcer repeated the same warnings over and over: "German planes are landing everywhere. Twelve unknown planes are nearing Soesterberg aerodrome. German Heinkels are circling above Rotterdam. German planes are dropping parachutists above Waalhaven aerodrome. From Schoonhoven parachutists' landings are announced. . . ." I immediately woke up my parents and told them the Germans had invaded our country. . . .

The confusion was incredible. Aerodromes were attacked; hangars, buildings and traffic towers fell. Clouds of parachutists floated over the heart of Holland, over dikes, cities and villages. On the isle of Dordrecht, an officer was awakened by his batman with the information that the isle was in German hands. He could not believe it, looked out of the window and saw that it was true. Another officer tried to phone his office and got a German on the phone. At 4 a.m. the army barracks in The Hague were bombed. Most of the soldiers inside, mainly young recruits of eighteen and nineteen years, were killed. There was heavy fighting on the roads. It was still so unreal to people that most went to their offices as usual at 8.30, though some could not make it, like friends of ours who had parachutists in their garden before breakfast. . . .

At 6 a.m., the minister of external affairs went to his department at the request of the German ambassador. Officially the war was still unknown to him, but on his way he had to take shelter several times. The German ambassador read him a document in typical Nazi style, accusing Holland of having conspired with England. In answer the minister took a pencil and wrote:

> The Dutch government rejects with indignation the accusation of the German government that it has, in any way or with any nation, made secret agreements directed against Germany. Taking into account the disgraceful German attack, an attack without any warning, the Dutch government considers that a state of war has now arisen between the Kingdom of the Netherlands and Germany.

It was 6.30 a.m. and Holland was officially at war with Germany. . . .

Dutch troops were encircled everywhere. Eastern Holland was practically taken on the first day. In the night, numerous people roamed over the roads on foot, carrying their most precious possessions. The third day was Whitsunday, a beautiful sunny day. Thousands of people flocked together in churches to pray for peace. Hospitals were overcrowded with wounded and dying soldiers and civilians. The official news bulletins were encouraging, but well-informed people knew that it was a hopeless fight against a superior and much stronger enemy.

The German front moved forward steadily; on the fourth day the heart of the Dutch defence system had already collapsed. . . . The next morning, May 14, we heard on the 8 a.m. broadcast that Queen Wilhelmina and the government had left. A proclamation of the Queen was read:

> After it had become absolutely certain that We and Our government in the Netherlands could not go on freely exercising our authority, the hard but necessary decision had to be taken to transfer the seat of government abroad for as long a time as is unavoidable, and with the intention of returning to Holland at the earliest possible opportunity. The government is now in England. It does not want to capitulate as a government.

When the Luftwaffe bombed Rotterdam, the old central area of the city was totally destroyed and the flames and smoke could be seen for miles around.

The proclamation finished:

> Do not despair. Do all that is possible in the clearly understood interest of the country. We do our part. Long live our Fatherland!

The effect of the proclamation was disastrous. Soldiers threw down their weapons, civilians cried. We felt deserted and the country was sunk in discouragement. . . .

At 10.30 a.m. the Dutch commander in Rotterdam received a German ultimatum to surrender or the city would be destroyed. At 1.30 p.m. the bombing started. The centre of the city was attacked systematically with explosive and fire bombs and went up in flames. Nothing remained. Hundreds of men, women and children died. Somebody said later: "Spring and death danced hand in hand in Rotterdam and when you saw it you felt completely removed from every normal sensation.". . . It was the end. They threatened to destroy other cities in like manner, so at 7.00 p.m. the commander-in-chief capitulated. Hurrying home towards eight, I saw people talking in groups everywhere. I went up to a friend of mine who, very quietly, said that we had capitulated. I did not believe it. We had been warned not to pay attention to such rumours. However, the radio confirmed it by reading the commander-in-chief's message to the German ambassador:

> I have to inform your excellency that the armed forces of the Netherlands, with the exception of the troops in Zeeland, lay down their arms in the face of the advancing German troops.

A moment later, our national anthem sounded for the last time through the radio. . . .

The next day they came, an endless stream of motorised units, armoured units, and artillery. The soldiers were well disciplined and looked sure of themselves. This massive display of military force made us realize how pitifully inadequate our efforts had been. We had never had a chance. Now we could only wait and see.

Vicki Tassie,
from *Life in Holland under German Occupation, 1940-45*

In September 1944 the British and American flags were raised over Antwerp after its liberation by British troops. The Allies hoped to use the port to ship in supplies for the invasion of Germany but could not do so as long as the fifty miles of river between Antwerp and the open sea were in German hands. The arduous task of clearing the approaches to the port was assigned to the Canadians.

14

Chapter One

Canada, the Netherlands and the War, 1939-1944

Canada and the Netherlands were less than likely allies. Canadians found themselves at war in 1939 not because their country had been attacked but because Britain had gone to war. The German invasion of Poland on September 1 led to a British ultimatum and, on September 3, a declaration of war. France followed suit six hours later. In Canada the rights and wrongs of the dispute between Poland and Germany seemed less significant than the fact that Britain was again locked in conflict with a powerful enemy. What most Canadians knew of Nazi Germany, moreover, they found repugnant. Canada's own declaration of war on September 10 was a foregone conclusion: "By Britain's side, whate'er betide." For the second time in twenty-five years Canadians readied themselves to fight in Europe.

On the other side of the Atlantic Ocean, the Netherlands mobilized its underequipped armed forces and prepared its defences. Not that the country expected to go to war: it opted for neutrality as it had in 1914-18. Small and weak, with a vulnerable colonial empire, it had no wish for war with any of its neighbours, and certainly not with Germany. Dutch relations with that country were generally good, even after Adolf Hitler came to power in 1933. There were close personal ties across the border, from the royal family on down. Queen Wilhelmina's mother was German; so was her husband. In 1937 Crown Princess Juliana married the German Prince Bernhard von Lippe-Biesterfeld. Commercial and business ties were also close: the wealth of the port of Rotterdam owed much to the transit trade with the industries of the German Ruhr valley. German was widely spoken in the Netherlands; the two languages are quite closely akin.

Early Dutch reactions to the Nazi regime in Germany were mixed. Some noted the tales of anti-Semitism and oppression told by Jewish and other refugees and deplored the obvious illiberalism of the new Germany. Others found things to admire there, the discipline and the decline in unemployment. The Netherlands and its main colony, the Dutch East Indies, were hard hit in the Depression. Economic distress no doubt contributed to the eight percent of the popular vote gained by the NSB, the Dutch national socialist movement, in the 1935 elections for the Provincial Estates. In this, the first elections in which it participated, the NSB became suddenly the fifth largest party.

Led by an engineer, Anton Mussert, the NSB drew most of its support from the *petite bourgeoisie* and the unemployed, those who felt menaced by the changing economy or who believed themselves its victims. But the aggressiveness of the NSB and its references to pagan, Germanic symbols worried the major churches. In 1936 both the Roman Catholic and Reformed churches denounced the NSB as anti-Christian. Secular groups also warned against the dangers of fascism. In the elections for the Estates General in 1937 the NSB share of the vote dropped to just under four percent. By 1939 the party was an unpopular minority, and after the outbreak of war in September a suspect one at that.

By 1939, too, the great majority of Netherlanders disapproved of the Nazi regime in Germany and feared it. Their hope was that they would not be attacked. They had good reason for that hope. With a little over nine million people occupying an area roughly the size of Vancouver Island, the Netherlands was not easy to defend. Dutch strategy, in the event of a German attack, would be to withdraw into the western and central parts of the country, "Fortress Holland," whose defensive lines would be flooded areas. The army would hold these lines until relief came, presumably from the British. The army, however, though far from negligible on paper—ten divisions—was undertrained and badly equipped. The air force had only 52 modern airplanes. The navy was stronger but a large part was stationed overseas. On the whole there had been little willingness in the inter-war years to spend money on the armed forces—in this respect the histories of the Netherlands and Canada were very similar. And perhaps the only sensible thing a tiny country could do was hope for peace.

There were several indications during the first winter of the war, the Phony War or *Sitzkrieg* as this period became known, that Hitler had designs on the Netherlands. But while Dutch military intelligence in Berlin was excellent it had little effect on Dutch policy. The military attaché in the Netherlands embassy in Berlin, Major G.J. Sas, was in contact with Colonel Hans Oster, deputy chief of German counter-espionage and a secret anti-Nazi. Sas was able to warn the Dutch government in The Hague several times of impending action against the Netherlands. As such action was repeatedly postponed, however, Major Sas's information came to be treated with growing scepticism. And his warnings were in any event insufficient to lead the government into a defensive alliance with Britain and France; it would not do to provoke Germany! As for the man in the street, he knew nothing of German plans. What he heard about them was based on wishful thinking: whatever Germany did, the Netherlands would escape invasion; its neutrality would be honoured, just as it had been in the 1914-18 war.

Early in the morning of May 10, 1940, a shocked nation realized that its neutrality had been brutally ended. Without a declaration of war—Hitler wanted total surprise—German armour smashed across the eastern frontier while bombers attacked Dutch airfields. Soon airborne troops were dropped near key objectives in the western Netherlands. Three of these were airfields in the neighbourhood of The Hague; the intention was to move quickly into the administrative centre and seize the royal family, members of the government, and the Dutch commander-in-chief, General H.G. Winkelman. This bold attempt failed, but elsewhere the Germans scored spectacular successes. The capture of the bridges at Rotterdam, Dordrecht and, above all, across the wide Hollands Diep at Moerdijk meant that, almost from the beginning, crucial points on the road into "Fortress Holland" were in German hands.

The enemy advanced quickly on a wide front. On May 14 the centre of Rotterdam was bombed. The result of a failure in German communications, the raid took almost a thousand Dutch lives. Allied propaganda would inflate this figure enormously; the bombing seemed one of the more startling examples of German terror. By this time the royal family and government had fled to England. Queen Wilhelmina especially had taken this step unwillingly; to this doughty widow it seemed as if she were abandoning her people in their hour of greatest need. However, the Dutch military situation had become hopeless. If the Queen and her ministers were not to be captured, their departure could not be delayed. When the people heard this news they were shocked; an even greater shock soon followed. Faced with the threat that the city of Utrecht would be bombed next, General Winkelman late on May 14 agreed to a capitulation. Only in the extreme southwest, in the province of Zeeland, did fighting rage for a few more days.

A conquered country had to adjust to German occupation. The Germans, led in the Netherlands by *Reichskommissar* Arthur Seyss-Inquart, hoped initially that most Netherlanders could be induced to recognize a community of interest with their "Aryan brethren." This hope soon turned out to be false. The general strike in Amsterdam in February 1941, directed against the occupation and against the growing persecution of the Jews, was an important event for both Netherlanders and their German overlords. Henceforth the repression of the civilian population, mainly carried out by the various Nazi police forces, became ever harsher. Particularly horrifying was the assault on the more than 130,000 Jews. Progressively isolated from the rest of Dutch society, most of them were eventually deported to the death camps in occupied Poland. In many other ways the Dutch people were terrorized. Their country was robbed, its industries and workers exploited for the benefit of the German war effort.

Demoralizing was the presence of a number of Dutch Nazis and collaborators. The proportion of the people who made common cause with the enemy was small: five percent or less. But some of this group were highly visible. Uniformed Dutch Nazis participated in the attacks on the Jews; after June 1941, others volunteered for duty on the new Russian front in the so-called Netherlands Legion. Although the Germans did not take the NSB or its leader, Mussert, very seriously and firmly refused to give it a share of government, they did encourage the entry of its members into important

In the aftermath of the bombing and the Dutch surrender, German troops in large numbers moved in to occupy Rotterdam and the other great urban centres of the western Netherlands.

For many Dutch citizens, the roundup and deportation of the Jews was one of the most traumatic events of the years of occupation. Many Dutch risked their lives by helping Jews to escape when escape was still possible, and later by providing Jews with hiding places or false identification papers.

War Documentation Centre (RIOD), Amsterdam

positions in the civil service, trade organizations and the like. A good many businessmen turned with alacrity to supply the Germans with goods and services, often at great profit to themselves. These people did not join the NSB, but they presumably thought the Germans were in the Netherlands to stay. In almost all walks of life, indeed, there were people who actively or passively sympathized with the enemy.

The bulk of the Dutch population, although deeply offended by the German presence, was more or less passive. They hoped for an Allied victory and sought to survive, living as normal a life as was possible under the circumstances. A growing number, however, joined one of several resistance groups. These necessarily operated "underground"—Dutch topography did not lend itself to guerrilla warfare. Some provided aid to *onderduikers*, literally "submerged ones," people who had gone into hiding from the Germans. Others helped downed Allied airmen to find their way to neutral soil and thence back to Britain; others again were involved in espionage or sabotage. Resistance groups printed and distributed illegal newspapers, because the sanctioned media were completely under German control.

Resistance activities prompted reprisals from the occupation authorities, reprisals that became increasingly brutal as the war went on. Not only were resistance figures, once apprehended, tortured and often executed, but men and women suspected of working with the resistance were put into preventive detention. Objectionable too was the taking of hostages, the detention of prominent citizens in the hope of thus controlling the population. At the same time the country became steadily poorer and life ever harder especially for those of modest means. The Netherlands in May 1940 had entered a nightmare that went on and on. It lasted more than four years in the three southern provinces, almost five years to the day in the eight provinces north of the great rivers.

By contrast the domestic experience of Canadians was tranquil. Sharing that relative tranquillity was the Dutch crown princess, Juliana, and her two daughters. A third daughter was born in Ottawa in 1943. They lived at Stornoway, now the house of the Leader of the Opposition, and in many ways were indistinguishable from Canadian families. Like many of the latter they had a husband and father overseas: Prince Bernhard was commander of the Netherlands Armed Forces and was in London much of the time. Also in the British capital was Juliana's mother, the sexagenarian Queen

As the occupation continued, the Dutch felt increasingly that they were being robbed by the Germans, that their country was being systematically looted. In this illustration from a series created by a Dutch artist in 1945, German soldiers are depicted seizing bicycles which had become the sole means of personal transportation.

AUG. V.D. LINDE / ORIGINALLY PUBLISHED BY DRUK VERSLUYS & SCHERJON, UTRECHT

Wilhelmina. She was head of the Dutch government-in-exile; through her frequent radio broadcasts she sought to encourage her sorely troubled people.

Although Canadian economic contributions to the Allied war effort were massive, Canadian military participation in the war was until the summer of 1942 largely limited to the air and the North Atlantic. The 1st Infantry Brigade had been transported to northern France in June 1940 then withdrawn before seeing action. For the next two years the number of Canadian soldiers in Britain grew without any units being committed to the fighting war. The Dieppe Raid in August 1942 was an ill-starred and tragic foray onto the Continent; it failed amidst heavy loss of life to the participating units of the 2nd Infantry Division. Not until the invasion of Sicily in the summer of 1943 did the soldiers of the Canadian Army feel that they were participating fully in the war.

For a year the interest of many Canadians focused on Italy, where the 1st Canadian Corps was part of the Allied force that was gradually pushing back the Germans. Comprising the 1st Infantry Division, 1st Army Tank Brigade and 5th Armoured Division, the corps saw frequently vicious action at places like Potenza and Ortona, at the Biferno and Moro Rivers, on the Gustav, the Hitler, and the Gothic Lines.

To the inhabitants of the Netherlands, however, as to many other Europeans, hope and fear both centred on the promised "Second Front" in western Europe. Italy was a long way off, the Russian front even farther. What they craved was an invasion in France, Belgium, possibly even the Netherlands. Only an assault in the west seemed

The ties between the Dutch and Canadian peoples were reinforced by the presence in Canada during the war of Princess Juliana and her children. The Princess' third daughter was born in Ottawa in January 1943. The birth raised the problem of a potential heiress to the Dutch throne being born in a foreign country, but this was solved by the Canadian government declaration beforehand that the place of birth, wherever it would be, would be considered extra-territorial. The christening of Juliana's daughter took place at St. Andrews Church in Ottawa in June and was attended by the child's grandmother, Queen Wilhelmina, Prime Minister Mackenzie King, and other Dutch and Canadian dignitaries.

likely soon to end the Nazi oppression. Hidden with her family in the "Achterhuis" on the Prinsengracht in Amsterdam, Anne Frank wrote in her diary on May 22, 1944: "It's no exaggeration to say that all Amsterdam, all Holland, yes, the whole west coast of Europe, right down to Spain, talks about the invasion day and night, debates about it, and makes bets on it and . . . hopes." She was surely right. Conditions in the Netherlands were deteriorating: rations of food and fuel decreased gradually, goods of most kinds were ever harder to obtain even in the black market, repression became more brutal.

On June 6, 1944—D-Day—the long-awaited invasion took place. Among the soldiers who waded ashore in Normandy that Tuesday morning and headed inland were the men of the 3rd Canadian Infantry Division. Several weeks of hard fighting ensued before the German resistance in Normandy collapsed and the Allies pushed into central and northern France. In July and August, the First Canadian Army took the city of Caen and helped close the Falaise Gap, an operation which cost the Germans tremendous losses of manpower and weapons. Consisting mainly of the 2nd and 3rd Infantry Divisions, 4th Armoured Division, 2nd Armoured Brigade, and 1st Polish Armoured Division, the First Canadian Army was on the left flank of the Allied advance as it turned north. Crossing the Seine near Rouen in late August, and liberating that city on August 30, the Canadians entered Dieppe again on September 1, victoriously this time.

Further to the east, American and French units had liberated Paris on August 25. Troops of the 30th British Corps entered Brussels on September 3 and the all-important port of Antwerp on September 4. The Germans were on the run.

So, on "Mad Tuesday," September 5, were many Dutch Nazis. The rapid Allied advance gave rise to wild rumours, according to which British troops had entered Breda in the province of North Brabant, even Arnhem, in Gelderland and thus north of the great rivers. Who could say Rotterdam, The Hague, Utrecht and Amsterdam might not be liberated within days? Long columns of German soldiers, joined by civilians, both German and Dutch, were moving north and east. Railway carriages of trains heading for Germany were packed. Impatiently Netherlanders waited for the arrival of the Allied advance units. Alas, many would have to wait for nine more months; some would never see them.

The Allied push had come to a temporary halt. By early September the supply lines stretched all the way from Normandy. Indeed, Antwerp figured prominently in plans to shorten them. Troubled by shortages of supplies, the British 11th Armoured Division failed to advance northwards from Antwerp after September 4. Most of the German Fifteenth Army was thus able to escape from Flanders along the waterways and roads of Zeeland. This in turn contributed to the failure of the Anglo-American Operation "Market-Garden," the attempt by means of a series of airborne attacks, co-ordinated with an armoured thrust, to seize three major bridges in the Netherlands: across the Maas at Grave, the Waal at Nijmegen, and the Neder Rijn at Arnhem. The operation began on September 17; the bridges at Grave and Nijmegen did fall into Allied hands. But the one at Arnhem did not. It was "a bridge too far." Survivors of the 1st British Airborne Division were evacuated from the north bank of the Neder Rijn on the night of September 25-26. "As it turned out," the eminent military historian C.P. Stacey

Public Archives Canada, DND 39776

Thousands of French citizens turned out to greet Canadian troops who returned to Dieppe victoriously in September 1944, about two years after the ill-fated raid which cost so many Canadian lives.

Public Archives Canada, DND 39575 / Ken Bell

Members of the Royal Hamilton Light Infantry visit the grave sites of regimental comrades who fell in the Dieppe raid in 1942.

writes, "the only hope of capturing the Ruhr in 1944 was lost with the Arnhem bridgehead."

In the meantime the First Canadian Army had not been idle. On September 3 Field Marshal Montgomery had assigned it the tasks of clearing the coastal belt and the towns of West Flanders. Spearheaded by the 1st Polish Armoured Division, the Canadians advanced. They crossed the Franco-Belgian border on September 6 and liberated Ypres. By the eleventh the Poles had reached Ghent. Further west, elements of the 2nd and 3rd Divisions laid siege to Boulogne, Calais and Dunkirk, and on September 9 occupied the port of Ostend. The Germans withdrew from the gorgeous town of Bruges without contesting possession, and on September 12 the 18th Armoured Car Regiment entered it, greeted by the cheers of an enthusiastic population.

The stage was set for the battle of the Scheldt. The largely undamaged facilities of Antwerp were unusable so long as the Germans controlled the river for the fifty miles between the port and the North Sea. On September 13 Montgomery told General H.D.G. Crerar, the officer commanding the First Canadian Army, that it was vital to clear the lower Scheldt, and assigned the task to the Canadians.

The liberation of the Netherlands began on that same day. In the southeast the capital city of the province of Limburg, Maastricht, was entered by units of the First U.S. Army. A week later the industrial city of Eindhoven, headquarters of the Philips company, was liberated by the American 101st Airborne Division as part of Operation "Market-Garden." On the day that operation began, September 17, the 1st Polish Armoured Division liberated Hulst in Zeeuws Vlaanderen and on the 20th the town of Terneuzen on the West Scheldt. They were soon afterwards joined by the Argyll and Sutherland Highlanders of Canada (Princess Louise's) of the 4th Armoured Division. There they halted, for the area to the west, soon to be known as the Breskens Pocket, was singularly unsuited to armoured warfare. Low-lying and wet, the terrain forced vehicles to take to the roads, usually located on top of the dikes. There they were extremely vulnerable to the German anti-tank guns, the dreaded 88s. No, this was infantry country if it was anything. In the weeks to come the men of the 3rd Division would learn to hate it.

In late September the 2nd Division began operations northeast of Antwerp in preparation for the push north. Further to the east the 1st British Corps was set in motion towards 's Hertogenbosch, the capital of North Brabant, in order to reduce the pressure on the left flank of the Second British Army. The high priority given to this in Field Marshall Montgomery's instructions of September 27, however, meant that the effort to clear the Scheldt came to rest almost entirely on the shoulders of the 2nd and 3rd Canadian Divisions. The assignment would turn out to be a heavy one.

On its entire front the First Canadian Army met strong resistance. The Germans were fully aware of the crucial importance of the downstream approaches to Antwerp; the line Antwerp-Tilburg-'s Hertogenbosch had to be held as long as possible. Most important of all at this stage, to both sides, was control of the South Beveland isthmus west of the small town of Woensdrecht. Thrusting north from Antwerp with the rest of the 2nd Division on October 2, the Calgary Highlanders of the 5th Brigade got into Hoogerheide, about a mile from Woensdrecht, on October 7. Ten days of attack and counterattack followed. Every yard taken by the Canadians the Germans contested;

In the first days of October 1944, the 2nd Canadian Infantry Division began its push northward from Antwerp. As the Canadians crossed into the Netherlands, the advance of armoured units was slowed down by the sodden condition of Dutch roads.

The fighting in the southern Netherlands intensified throughout October 1944. As the Canadians advanced, Dutch refugees could be seen fleeing along dikes in flooded areas of the countryside.

often they took it back. Crack troops, the so-called "Battle Group Chill," sought, ultimately in vain, to deny the isthmus to the skilful and tenacious Canadians. Not until October 16 did the Royal Hamilton Light Infantry manage to dislodge the defenders from Woensdrecht. Strong artillery support materially helped to defeat the desperately determined Germans; at one point the RHLI called down Canadian fire on its own positions to catch the exposed Germans during one of their counterattacks. The fire was pinpoint accurate; the enemy had to retreat.

In the course of the battle for Woensdrecht, the importance of the Scheldt operation had been further upgraded by Montgomery. All Allied units were feeling the lack of a major port nearer to the battle lines than Normandy was; on October 9 Montgomery gave absolute priority within the First Canadian Army to the opening of Antwerp. The following day General Eisenhower offered to make American troops available if this might speed the process. The 104th U.S. Infantry Division was soon afterwards made part of the First Canadian Army, the first time in history that an American division had served under Canadian command.

On October 20 an attack began, involving divisions of four different nationalities, which was intended to loosen support for the German positions in Zeeland. From west to east, the 4th Canadian Armoured Division thrust towards Bergen op Zoom, the English 49th (West Riding) Infantry Division pushed towards Roosendaal, the 104th U.S. Division headed north between Roosendaal and Breda, and the Polish Armoured Division, with the 2nd Canadian Armoured Brigade on its left, set course for Breda. That historic old garrison town, made famous by Velasquez, fell to the Poles on October 29. Meanwhile the Second British Army had launched an attack on 's Hertogenbosch and Tilburg, liberating these two cities on October 24 and 28. On the twenty-seventh the 10th Canadian Infantry Brigade took Bergen op Zoom; gradually the German position in the province of North Brabant was being reduced. The U.S. 104th Division

Canadian forces were able to make a surprise attack on German troops concentrated in the Breskens pocket area on the south bank of the Scheldt river by launching an unexpected amphibious assault from the east across the Braakman Inlet.

reached the bridges at Moerdijk on November 8. But whereas these had fallen into German hands intact in May 1940, they had now been blown up by the retreating *Wehrmacht*. There was to be no easy passage for the Allies into "Fortress Holland."

Along the West Scheldt the Canadians had not stood still. The clearing of the Breskens Pocket from the south across the Leopold Canal and from the east across the Braakman inlet began on October 6 and 9 respectively, after the 3rd Division was again at full strength. (Not until October 1 had the German garrison at Calais capitulated.) Everywhere the resistance was what it had been expected to be: resourceful and tenacious. Fortunately the amphibious attack across the Braakman took the enemy by surprise, allowing the North Nova Scotia Highlanders and the Highland Light Infantry of Canada to establish a good beachhead before the Germans were able to direct effective shelling into the area. On both fronts the advance of the Canadians, reinforced by the 157th Brigade of the British 52nd (Lowland) Division and units of the 79th Armoured Division, was slow and painful but steady. The port of Breskens fell to the Stormont, Dundas and Glengarry Highlanders on October 21. Operation "Switchback," as the enterprise was known, came to an end on November 2-3, when the last strongpoints on the Dutch-Belgian border were taken. The Breskens Pocket was clear of Germans at last.

Like their comrades south of the West Scheldt, the men of the 2nd Division faced a hard task. Poised to enter South Beveland, they waited until October 24, when the threat of their right flank had been eliminated as a result of the advance of the 1st British Corps. Parts of the peninsula had been flooded by the Germans and, just as in the Breskens Pocket, the low-lying terrain was crisscrossed by drainage ditches. This difficult country combined with wellplaced German anti-tank guns to stymie the armoured units once again; the infantry, tired and short of men, would have to do the

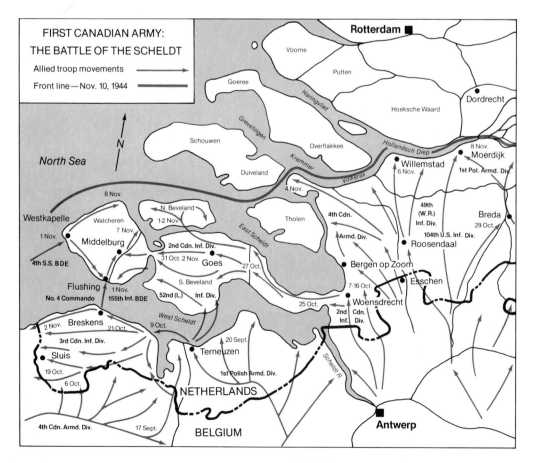

job. Supported by the artillery and the air forces, and assisted by an outflanking amphibious operation carried out by the 156th Brigade of the 52nd (Lowland) Division, the 6th Canadian Brigade crossed the Beveland Canal on October 26 and 27. The remaining Germans now retreated to the island of Walcheren; Goes, the largest town on South Beveland, was liberated by the Canadian Black Watch on October 29. A squadron of the 8th Reconnaissance Regiment took the small island of North Beveland on November 1 and 2.

The toughest nut remained to be cracked. Walcheren and its many gun emplacements commanded the entrance to the Scheldt. In preparation for the assault on the island, Bomber Command on October 3 breached the dike at Westkapelle. Much of the island was flooded as a result, significantly impairing the enemy's communications and lines of supply. But further bombing raids, carried out whenever weather permitted, had little effect on the German concrete coastal defences. Throughout their struggle in the Breskens Pocket, the men of the 3rd Division had reason to curse the heavy artillery located along the coast from Flushing to Westkapelle.

From October 31 to November 2 the battalions of the 5th Canadian Brigade attempted in turn to advance along the causeway, one kilometre long, that linked Walcheren to South Beveland. The losses were heavy. On the third day "D" company of Le Régiment de Maisonneuve managed to establish itself on the Walcheren side, and was then relieved by Scottish troops. It was the last action seen by Canadian infantry along the Scheldt. Amphibious landings on November 1 at Flushing and Westkapelle by the Royal Marines, the Inter-Allied Commandos, and the Scottish 155th Brigade, spelled the end of the German hold on Walcheren. The capital of Zeeland, Middelburg, showing the heavy damage it had sustained in May 1940, was liberated on November 6; the last German resistance on the island ended a couple of days later.

The wet conditions and flooding along the South Beveland peninsula made the movement of heavy vehicles difficult and hazardous.

The task of clearing mines from the West Scheldt downstream from Antwerp had already started. On November 26 the Royal Navy finished the job; two days later the first convoy entered the harbour of Antwerp. The Allies had the great supply port in northwest Europe which they needed to prepare for the final assault on Germany. More than 6,300 Canadians had been killed and wounded in the effort to open it.

In the midst of the fighting it was encouraging to the troops to be reminded that they came as liberators. The welcome given by civilians was warm. "The men had to kiss babies and sign autographs all the way through town," the War Diary of the Canadian Black Watch noted in describing the liberation of Goes. But relief and joy were mixed with shock and grief, as civilians contemplated the damage done to their communities by military action or mourned those who had died. They and the soldiers both knew that the war was not yet over, that others would die before it ended.

When the Battle of the Scheldt and the associated offensive in North Brabant drew to a close early in November, the First Canadian Army was ready for a rest. The three Canadian divisions especially were exhausted. Fortunately for them, the war on the western front now entered a quiet period which provided an opportunity for recuperation. The Allies held a front that more or less followed the pre-war boundary of Germany with France and Belgium. In the north it corresponded closely to the Maas river, though in Limburg the Second British Army had not quite got that far while having gone beyond it in the Nijmegen salient. For the Dutch people the cardinal fact was that only a small part of the country had been liberated. The province of North Brabant and much of the provinces of Zeeland and Limburg now had the worst of the war behind them. For the rest of the Netherlands, including the most heavily populated areas, the greatest horrors had only just begun.

Tanks move toward the Beveland Canal, the major German defensive line across South Beveland. Once the Germans were defeated in the canal area, they retreated to Walcheren Island, and Canadian troops moved with relatively little difficulty across the rest of the peninsula.

A group of villagers in Krabbendijke watch Canadian troops advance through South Beveland toward the Beveland Canal.

German prisoners were put to work hauling logs for the construction of a new bridge being built by Canadian army engineers over the Beveland Canal.

Dutch children watch soldiers of the Fort Garry Horse fix a tank track.

In a field along the South Beveland causeway, Dutch civilians cut up for food cattle that were destroyed in the fighting.

Vicki Tassie

September 1944: Hope and Despair

DAVID KAUFMAN

Mrs. Vicki Tassie (née Hoeksma) was just out of university and living in The Hague at the outbreak of the war. Twenty-five years later, in Canada, she wrote a private memoir of life in Holland under German occupation. This excerpt, one of several in this book from that account, describes the emotional turmoil that swept the Netherlands in the fall of 1944.

On September 3, Brussels was a free city again. The next day the BBC interrupted its program to give the news that the Allies' armies had crossed the Dutch border. Our liberation was in sight now, and rumours started to flow. . . .

The general feeling that this was the last stage of the war became so suggestive that it triggered the phenomenon called "Mad Tuesday." It was a warm fall day, Tuesday the fifth of September. At the Red Cross, somebody told me that he had just telephoned the city of Breda in Brabant. They expected the Allies within half an hour. Then we heard that the south of Holland was already free. In The Hague it was said that the Allies had arrived in Rotterdam twelve miles to the south. In Haarlem they said that The Hague had been liberated. Everywhere people were standing along the roads with flowers and little flags to welcome the Allied troops; no one wanted to miss the excitement of seeing the first tanks of the liberation armies arrive. Panic gripped the Nazis who streamed to the stations to leave for Germany. . . . Men who had been in hiding came out. A resistance commando in Rotterdam took possession of the Hydro building, Nazi mayors were arrested in several places, and the town of Axel in Zeeland liberated itself. Hundreds of Germans surrendered there while the resistance occupied the town hall. Cafes were full of people celebrating with orange bitters (the national drink). It was just a matter of hours now, and a kind of carnival mood reigned in the streets. But nothing happened, and the next morning everything returned to "normal." Flags were hastily taken in, fugitives hid again, the SD [German security police] gradually came back, only the expectation remained. . . .

In those days, the first V-2s were shot off from The Hague, and to that purpose whole quarters were evacuated within twenty-four hours' notice. Streams of people were seen in the streets, carrying as much of their possessions as they could manage. When V-2s were fired, the sky would turn red and there was a tremendous noise as if a train were thundering through the skies, the sound slowly diminishing unless something went wrong. Then the noise would suddenly stop and the V-2 would come hurtling down, bringing destruction and death. There was always tension when one was fired; will the noise stop? And if it did, there was that fearful moment of waiting for the crash. It was one more thing to put up with, and we were becoming very impatient for the end.

Then came the third Sunday in September when the liberation of northern Holland seemed to be at hand for the second time. It was Sunday, September 17. For hours the sky was black with the armada of planes flying over, and perplexed, we wondered what was happening. In the afternoon, the word was passed around that there had been a radio bulletin: "Airborne troops are landing near Arnhem." Excitement began to rise again, and the expectant mood of Mad Tuesday returned.

Trusting that the whole country would soon be free, the Dutch government in London ordered the railways to strike, in order to dislocate German military traffic. At 5.45 p.m., the BBC Netherlands News carried the government's instructions and the same evening Radio Oranje gave the coded message "Uncle John's children have to go home." The instructions were promptly carried out. Railroaders, from the directors down to the engine cleaners, struck and the whole apparatus came to a standstill. All personnel went into hiding and on Monday not a single train moved.

It was hard to keep track of what was happening. While the Battle of Arnhem raged, German demolition units blew up the harbour installations of Amsterdam and Rotterdam. Cranes tumbled into the water, elevators were smashed, wharves and factories burned down. The machinery was attacked with sledge hammers. In Amsterdam alone over three hundred million guilders worth of equipment was blown sky high. The fighting

for Arnhem and Nijmegen went on for nine days which most of the residents spent in cellars, caught between British parachutists and German troops. . . .

The tension was nearly unbearable with freedom so close at hand. But alas, the attempt to liberate Holland at one stroke failed. On September 27, Radio London confirmed the failure and added that the people in northern Holland had before them months that would be counted among the most difficult in Holland's history as a nation. The disappointment was bitter and well it might be. The war front was now established right through the country, cutting the densely populated north off from the coal mines in the south. Trains could not transport food to the cities any more and the occupation authorities forbade food transportation by ship as a punitive measure against the railway strike.

Practically without fuel and with food supplies dwindling rapidly, we girded ourselves for the last stretch. The winter of 1944-45 was a nightmare which those who went through . . . will never forget. The Nazi regime, knowing that the game was up, took it out on the defenceless population which was to get intimately acquainted with terror and starvation before it would get its freedom. . . .

In the last year of the war, the Germans exacted a heavy toll in human lives and property through the use of V1 and V2 rockets against urban targets. The rockets not only brought death to the target centres—as seen here in a picture taken after an attack on Antwerp—but they often malfunctioned and exploded close to their launching sites, many of which were located in major cities in the Netherlands.

Ben Dunkelman

Along the Scheldt: An Enemy Terrain

When Canada declared war against Germany in 1939, Ben Dunkelman, a young Toronto Jew, decided he wanted to enlist in the struggle to defeat Hitler. However, as he recounts in his autobiography, Dual Allegiance, at that time "enlisting took on something of the character of trying to join an exclusive club." But he persisted and finally made it to Europe as an officer with the Queen's Own Rifles of Canada, who took part in the invasion on D-Day. Here he describes the problems that Canadian troops faced in their first, and most difficult, campaign in the Netherlands.

Early in September, Antwerp had been captured by General Dempsey's British Second Army, but there was one problem: the approaches to the port of Antwerp, the banks of the Scheldt estuary, had not been cleared. To the north, the river entrance was covered by the heavy German naval guns on Walcheren Island. To the south, the enemy

occupied the mainland area known as the Breskens Pocket, just north of the Leopold Canal. This area was crisscrossed with high dikes which were mined and surrounded by flooded polder fields and there were fourteen thousand crack troops of the German Sixty-fourth Division entrenched there. The Canadian troops of the Third Infantry Division had been involved in the fighting from D-Day on, and had participated in many heavy battles in the drive through Caen and Falaise, Boulogne and Calais, in France. We thought we were in for a bit of a rest, but the Americans were occupied in the south of France and had also participated with the British in the fighting at Nijmegen and Arnhem in the eastern Netherlands; so, it was the Third Division that was called in again to assault another fortress.

Montgomery had said that the terrain of the Scheldt estuary was abominable. The Belgian military staff had called it impossible ground for fighting. I must say that I remember the Scheldt estuary as a hell on earth for the soldier. Not only were the dikes mined but they were covered by German guns. To cross the polders that surrounded the dikes, we had to walk waist deep in ice-cold water under enemy fire. This was a task that no ordinary soldier could have been called on to perform. Later General Montgomery said that only superior troops of the highest calibre could have accomplished the task of taking this ground.

One of our greatest problems in the Breskens Pocket was communications. We would move forward over the flooded polders, get to our objective, fight our way onto it, and then find out that our radio sets were out of order. Because of this, those of us who had received training on motorcycles were called into action, to drive at top speed along the tops of dikes and carry communications and supplies to the troops. The motorcycles were well suited to this purpose because of their mobility on dikes and their ability to evade enemy fire. I can well recall trying to get up to my troops one day when a German tank sitting on the next dike over let loose at me with its heavy 88 mm and its 55 mm machine guns. I was racing along the dike, skidding back and forth, and to this day I don't know how I got through.

George Teasdale

South Beveland: A Soldier's Ordeal

While the 3rd Canadian Infantry Division was occupied with the clearance of the southern bank of the Scheldt estuary, the 2nd Division was sent up from Antwerp to clear the northern bank, consisting of the South Beveland peninsula and Walcheren Island which were connected by a causeway. The drive past Woensdrecht at the entrance to South Beveland, the push along South Beveland, and the attempt to secure a beachhead on Walcheren involved battles that were among the worst in the histories of several regiments.

George Anthony Teasdale tried to enlist in Toronto in 1940 but was rejected for medical reasons. He tried again, was successful, and went overseas in 1944. He was sent into the Netherlands with reinforcements for the Calgary Highlanders, and, after a two-week course in Antwerp, rejoined his company in October just as the regiment began its push across South Beveland.

Word filtered down that our company was going to attack a radar station. In preparation, I had scrounged a lot of ammunition. I still had a Sten gun and I loaded up with half a dozen grenades. My intuition told me that this was going to be a tough battle, and being left-handed, I felt better having the Sten because it was easier for me to operate than the rifle which most of the infantry carried. Early in the morning, we all lined up, and our officer yelled at someone in the back of the lines to get up front. The next thing we know, this piper comes up, which was very unusual, and everybody yells at him: "Let's go there, pipes." So the piper started playing his tune, and away we went.

Even at the starting point we were being sniped at, but, as far as I can remember, no one got hit then. The piper played perhaps for five minutes, and then ran back with everybody yelling, "Goodbye, you lucky. . ." We turned west along a highway and then started working our way across a polder. It was muddy and there was water all around us.

(Opposite) The soft ground and flooded fields of the Breskens pocket proved to be largely impassable for heavy equipment. The burden of clearing the area of the enemy fell mainly on the foot soldiers of the 3rd Canadian Infantry Division who came to be known as "water rats."

About eleven or twelve o'clock noon, we got to a rendezvous spot and were waiting for some grub when, all of a sudden, an 88 mm gun opened up on the carrier coming up behind us. At that point, we did not know that we were being observed constantly. The carrier finally made it and we dug into slit trenches. Just as we began to eat, we were fired on again and didn't get to touch the food. As soon as the firing stopped, we were up and away.

We went over a dike, through a Toronto Scottish machine gun emplacement which was firing continuously to the west, down the highway a bit, and then north across another polder. We expected to draw some small arms fire and didn't have to wait long. A German on top of a dike opened up on us and some guys were just cut in two. Well, we didn't have time to stop; we had to get on top of the dike and flush this guy out. But this stalled everything, and put the wind up the whole company. Some guys who were injured had fallen in the ditches and there was a lot of screaming. We walked on a bit farther, and we couldn't find anybody, but there were trenches all along the dike—beautiful German trenches with walls and straw, so we stopped there for the night.

Moving out the next morning, we picked up a lone sniper who we thought was responsible for the shooting the day before. Then we worked our way to the centre of a polder and took a few other snipers prisoner; they just gave up. A little trouble started here. Because of our experience of the day before, with the injuries and the screaming, everybody was uptight, and there was some pushing and shoving and hauling off with the fists. I got into the act, too, which was stupid, but we were all pretty upset. This broke up, then some of the guys wanted to shoot the prisoners, but all we did was intimidate them a bit.

We moved on toward a section of high ground which seemed to be our objective, but we still couldn't see any radar station. Then we doubled back towards a dike and started to dig in again. While we were digging, somebody yelled "25-pounders" and we could hear guns going off. In effect, we had gone too far. Down came our own artillery, but there weren't too many rounds and no damage was done. After that stopped and we were half dug in, we saw soldiers coming at us from the highway, carrying fixed bayonets. Our wireless set had given out, so we started to yell. They got within a hundred yards of us, stopped, and turned back. It was just another snafu.

We took off again, and eventually spotted a railway line that went east across the isthmus and north to Bergen op Zoom. We moved into the corner of the railway embankment and a large dike, and when we got on top of the dike,

George Teasdale, in a photograph taken in Belgium in 1944 (top), and today (left).

36

we could see a large barn directly ahead, with figures running around it, and the high ground off to our right. No sooner had the company spread out on top of the dike than down came the mortar. Luckily it was landing in soft ground and wasn't too effective. We opened up on the figures ahead of us, but then got caught in heavy machine gun cross-fire. Guys to my left and right were getting hit, and I couldn't shoot because the range of my gun was too short. So I rolled down the embankment. At the bottom I found one of my friends bleeding pretty badly, so I started to help him, but then the corporal came up, motioned at me with his weapon, and told me to get back on top of the dike. At this moment someone called for my section, so I ran and joined up with a sergeant and three other privates.

We had to get over the railway embankment which was quite steep. The machine guns were still pouring it on. The barn was straight ahead and I figured that was where the radar station was. No matter what the barn was, it must have been important because it was heavily defended. We got across to the base of the hill on our right; we knew the machine gun emplacement was on top and we had to knock it out. I took a few steps up the hill with two of the privates, then looked around, and saw the sergeant and the other private standing beside each other. It seemed clear that the sergeant was going to look after this guy. Next thing I know, the sergeant made a threatening gesture towards us and tells us to get on up the hill. Just like that. So I moved up.

I got to the crest and started crawling through low brush that was less than a foot high and provided practically no cover. I crawled and I crawled and the machine gun was still blasting away. I could see the barbed wire ahead, and a few figures. So I got up to the wire and let go all over the place with the Sten. In the back of my head, my mind is flying. I'm thinking maybe if I can fire in all directions, they'll think there are more of us than there actually are. My mind was just exploding. I heaved a couple of grenades and then let go a few more bursts of the Sten. The machine gun stopped and it got awfully quiet.

A moment later, one of the guys crawled up

Soldiers of the Calgary Highlanders march past ruined houses along a wet road in South Beveland.

beside me and told me that the barbed wire on the right ended and turned a corner. To the left, the barbed wire stretched as far as I could see. He told me to keep firing while he worked his way around the corner. I told him not to do it but to stay with me. He had a rifle, which was difficult to fire while crawling, and no grenades, but away he went. I didn't know what effect my grenades had had, but I assumed the Germans were scared too. The guy got to the corner of the wire fence and disappeared. I'm looking and listening, and there is not a shot, not a word—nothing. By this time, the other private had crawled up beside me looking for his buddy. I also told him to stay put, but away he went, and the same thing happened—he disappeared.

I stayed there until it got dark then crawled back a bit. I couldn't dig into the hill because the ground was too hard, so I lay there and the night passed. The next morning I was still lying there when I heard a loud bang. I looked around and here was a tank that had pulled up firing shells right over my head. I raised my arm and moved the Sten up and down a few times, and the tank stopped firing, backed off, and pulled away. Another day went by and nothing happened. I kept thinking there would be a counter attack but it never came. I didn't know what was going on at the bottom of the hill. Where was everybody? I don't know why I stayed put.

I stayed on the hill another night. During the next day, at one point I heard footsteps coming up behind me. I looked around and there was some guy running up the hill with a grenade in his hand—he was one of ours. He had no helmet on and looked angry. He ran past me, up to the fence, and there was one shot. He stopped, turned around, and I could see he was hit right between the eyes. He walked right past me, still holding the grenade, and his momentum carried him back to the brow of the hill. There was no explosion. He was a dead man. That was the third day.

The fourth day, somebody came halfway up the hill and started to dig in. It was a lieutenant and several privates from my regiment. I could hear them arguing and I went down to take a look, but just then the Germans tossed some stick grenades at us and I went back to the top where I figured it was

safer. All the time I kept thinking I was being observed, but except for those grenades, there had been no more fire. That night some soldiers set up three Bren guns below the brow of the hill, so I joined them and we dug in a bit. During the night we heard noises. The Germans couldn't hold this place because they were being cut off, and it was obvious that they were finally pulling out.

The next morning it was all over, and everybody disappeared. I was still curious about the two guys who had gone around the fence at the top, so I went back up to have a look. There was a concrete hole where the machine guns were, and I spotted the two guys. They were face down on the ground, spread-eagled. I didn't touch them in case they had been booby-trapped. All I could do was look. They had been shot in the base of the skull. I ran down the hill and reported my findings to the commanding officer. I also ran into that sergeant. He was surprised to see me.

I got back into my company, but there weren't many of us left. We regrouped with other soldiers in the regiment, and my name was called to go out on a fighting patrol with thirty or forty other guys. As we left, we could see smoke and flames rising from the burning barn. We walked about a mile. There was a lot of debris strewn around—overturned carts and dead horses, and we passed three freshly dug graves with crosses. But there was no activity. I hated patrols because you never knew what to expect.

Later we went back to a town, washed up, and stayed there overnight. The next morning we were off again, and we walked until we reached the South Beveland town of Goes. The whole brigade was there and tanks had moved up. The civilians were out, and we

Dutch children wave to passing tanks of the 4th Canadian Armoured Division as troops enter the town of Bergen-op-Zoom.

gave them cigarettes, and chocolate to the kids. Later we left Goes and walked all night to the west. We had to be damn careful because of the booby-traps in the road, and all the time we were being urged on by the officer we liked to call the Mad Major. In the morning we continued on to Walcheren Island and we eventually reached the causeway joining it to South Beveland.

The next day, after the rest of the regiment came up, we moved to the entrance of the causeway. A lot of the young kids were getting upset. It was pretty awesome. The Germans were firing shells from the other end, bouncing them off the road, and they were ricocheting back and forth all over the place. But the attack had begun. We moved out early in the morning, onto the road, and found a lot of dead bodies from the regiment that had been in ahead of us. As soon as we started to run, the firing began, and I can still remember the Mad Major yelling, "Come on, you sons-of-bitches!" We got all separated. At one point, an armoured bulldozer came along to try to fill in a ditch that had been blasted across the centre of the causeway, but it drew heavy fire and had to back off.

I think I got close to the other side, but I don't know how close. When I had worked my way forward, I jumped into a crater and found a major from another company. There were a half dozen bodies lying in the hole. The major asked me who I was and where I had come from. When he saw me peering over the edge, he told me to stay put. We talked a bit about the attack, and he was obviously upset. Things had gone wrong.

After a while, my own company's commanding officer and a platoon lieutenant crawled up beside us. They looked into the crater, spotted me and the major, and yelled at us to go with them. The major grabbed my shoulder and told me again to stay where I was. The other officers went on. The next thing I know, there was a hell of a commotion and back they came, both of them hurt, dragging each other. That's how far they had gone. We couldn't move ahead. Anyway, the battle lasted the whole day, and when the night came, somebody crawled up beside us to call us back. I remember getting off the causeway—I was out of it. We were a sorry looking bunch.

T.M. Hunter

Excerpts from a War Diary

Captain T. Murray Hunter, now with the history department of Carleton University, was the historical officer at 2nd Division headquarters. These brief excerpts from his war diary highlight the contradictions and concerns felt by soldiers at the time: the relative ease of life in newly liberated Antwerp which was still separated from the front by only a few miles; the dangerous inability of the Germans to control their powerful rocket weapons; the burning concern over the quality of reinforcements; and the most important question—when would it all end?

October 13, 1944

Houses in ruins, mine craters along the road, with extensive mine fields on either side still bearing warning signs in both German and English, and wrecked vehicles all marked the progress of the struggle north of Antwerp.

Antwerp provided many points of particular interest to anyone recently arrived from the United Kingdom. In general the people on the streets of the city appeared to be rather

T. Murray Hunter.

DAVID KAUFMAN

better dressed than the British people. This contrast was sharply defined insofar as women's dress was concerned. The shop windows exhibited an extensive variety of goods and there were many articles, certainly in the electrical line, that one would not expect to find so conspicuous in English shops. It was also remarkable that there were a number of comparatively new American automobiles, including Buicks and Chevrolets, in the streets. Some of these appeared to be owned by civilians. After the "lean" years in Britain—where fruit such as grapes, when obtainable, sold for seventeen shillings and a sixpence a pound—it was a great treat to be able to buy a kilogram of grapes for approximately twenty-five francs in Antwerp. Another noticeable feature of the city was the number of American cinema pictures that were being shown.

October 14, 1944

During the day, a visit was paid to the scene of the flying-bomb accident near Eeckeren. This bomb had the unfortunate effect of destroying all equipment of the 2nd Canadian Infantry Division Mobile Laundry. At the time of the accident, this unit had been functioning in an open meadow, and total casualties included six Other Ranks killed, nineteen wounded. The four large vehicles being used by the laundry were almost completely destroyed and the crater, which was no more than twenty-five yards from the vehicles, was fifty feet wide and about seven or eight feet deep. Under the circumstances, it was perhaps fortunate that the bomb had fallen on soft ground and had penetrated as far as it did before exploding. Later in the afternoon, the detachment received a routine notice that there would be no exchange of clothing at bath parades until further notice. During the day, a number of peculiarly sharp explosions were heard and these resembled very closely those that had been attributed to rockets in London in recent weeks.

October 15, 1944: On a visit to The Black Watch (Royal Highland Regiment) of Canada

At this time, the battalion was at rest, in and about a large farmhouse, recuperating from an

Three Canadian soldiers purchase grapes from a Belgian fruit vendor in the Breskens pocket area.

PUBLIC ARCHIVES CANADA, DND 41734 / D.I. GRANT

intensive period of fighting during the previous forty-eight hours. . . . Obviously this unit had been engaged in severe fighting, and the Intelligence Officer had some very bitter and pointed remarks to make concerning the quality of reinforcements. From this and other sources, the problem of reinforcements with inadequate infantry training appears to be a very serious matter in this division.

October 22, 1944: On a visit to the Royal Hamilton Light Infantry

In common with other units recently visited, RHLI were extremely bitter over the quality of reinforcements received. The opinion of the second-in-command and the company commanders was unanimous on this point. During the previous five days of fighting, the battalion had suffered approximately a hundred and eighty-five casualties and were ten officers under strength.

November 6, 1944: On a lecture by Lt.-Gen. Guy Simonds, Acting Commander of the First Canadian Army

He revealed that the 2nd Division had per-formed the operations allotted to it on the South Beveland peninsula by the target date of the first of November.

Dealing with the question of whether the war with Germany would end in 1944, he said that two important questions arose: First, would the weather hold long enough for the Allies to finish before the end of the year? Second, would the enemy fight the decisive Battle of Germany west of the Rhine? In his words, if the enemy decided to fight west of the Rhine, "I believe he can be defeated before the turn of the year." Nevertheless he added: "If the bridges across the Rhine were blown, and if the enemy retired to the right bank, in all probability there would be a spring campaign."

At the conclusion of his address, the acting Army Commander had some remarks to make with respect to the reinforcement situation. He stressed the fact that, in dealing with these reinforcements, officers and NCOs would be required to take special care to make them feel that they were part of their respective units during the limited period available before active operations continued.

The Black Watch (Royal Highland Regiment) of Canada suffered terribly high casualties in the drive to seal off the entrance to the South Beveland peninsula at Woensdrecht. Some of the soldiers who died in the assault were buried during this ceremony at Ossendrecht, a few miles south of the entrance to South Beveland.

PUBLIC ARCHIVES CANADA, DND 41902 / KEN BELL

(Opposite) Soldiers of the 2nd Canadian Armoured Brigade parade through Breda on November 2, 1944, to mark the occasion of the entry of Canadian troops into the Netherlands.

(Above) A soldier from a reconnaissance unit with children from the town of Oostkerke in South Beveland.

(Left) A soldier of the Fort Garry Horse shows photographic snapshots to a woman dressed in traditional costume in the town of Goes in South Beveland. This photograph and other similar ones were apparently taken by Canadian army photographers at the request of the Kodak Company of Canada.

Public Archives Canada, DND 42949 / M.M. Dean

*In the late summer of 1944,
as the Allied troops sped
across France, there had been
some hope that the war would
end that year, but as months
passed, it became clear that
the troops would have to
spend another winter overseas
before the final push into
Germany. Here, a Canadian
soldier reads a sign on the
road to Nijmegen, and
contemplates the approaching
Christmas season.*

Chapter Two

The Long Winter

On November 10, 1944, the 2nd Canadian Corps took over the Nijmegen salient from the 30th British Corps. The salient, a narrow prong of territory, was a legacy of Operation "Market-Garden;" it extended northwards from the ancient city of Nijmegen to the village of Heteren on the Neder Rijn. It was to this point that six weeks earlier the surviving remnants of the 1st British Airborne Division had been ferried from Oosterbeek across the river. Two British infantry divisions, the 49th (West Riding) and the 51st (Highland) took over the salient itself; the 2nd and 3rd Canadian divisions were in a line from west to southeast of Nijmegen. The other half of the First Canadian Army, the 1st British Corps, held the line downstream along the Maas and to the tip of Walcheren. Thus the 4th Canadian Armoured Division was strung out north and west of the capital of North Brabant, 's Hertogenbosch. And some Canadian units were still besieging Dunkirk, whose garrison was not to surrender until the following May.

The salient was well within the range of the German artillery. The land was low, moreover, and in constant danger of being flooded. One task carried out by the Canadians was the evacuation of the civilians from the area. Many of them went with heavy heart. Even when the dangers of staying are clear there may be little desire to leave home. The Germans did flood the plain in conjunction with a sharp local attack on December 4. It was repulsed, but the flooding led to a minor withdrawal of British units and a shortening of the line north of Nijmegen.

For the next few weeks the most important task of the 2nd Canadian Corps was to ensure that the enemy did not recapture or destroy the two Waal bridges at Nijmegen. As the Waal is the largest stream in the Rhine delta, the bridges loomed large in planning for the future. Recognizing this, the Germans tried repeatedly to destroy them. Mines were floated down the river in November and December; some of them caused damage before a protective boom was constructed upstream by Canadian Engineers. A midget submarine attack on January 13 failed amidst a Canadian artillery barrage in which the 12th and 14th Field Regiments RCA and the anti-tunk guns of the Stormont, Dundas and Glengarry Highlanders all participated. The bridges continued to stand.

On the whole life in the line was relatively quiet until February. Not that the troops relaxed greatly; the menace of a German counterattack, such as the Ardennes offensive in late December, was never far from anyone's mind. There was an occasional local action, notably the vicious fighting at Kapelsche Veer on the Maas east of Geertruidenberg, in the closing days of January. Primarily of symbolic significance, the elimination of the small bridgehead cost the Lincoln and Welland Regiment 179 casualties, the Argyll and Sutherland Highlanders of Canada 48, and the South Alberta Regiment seven. Enemy losses were about the same. However, until the push into the Rhineland began on February 8, most Canadian soldiers in northwest Europe had a chilly but uneventful three months. This respite was precious, for it allowed units to recover from the losses incurred in the clearing of the Scheldt and men to overcome the physical and mental exhaustion which that operation had produced.

The campaign that had begun with the invasion of Normandy and had continued without pause until it ground to a temporary halt in November had created a manpower problem for the Canadian Army. Added to the losses of Italy, where the 1st Canadian Corps was still battling its way forward, the drive from Normandy into the Low Countries had resulted in heavy casualties, some 34,000 by the end of September. The infantry in particular had suffered greater losses than had been anticipated, and it was in this branch of the service that there was a shortage of replacements. During the Battle of the Scheldt many of the regiments were short of troops, which affected their effectiveness significantly.

For the second time in the war, conscription for overseas military service became a burning issue. In the winter of 1942 Prime Minister William Lyon Mackenzie King had managed nimbly to sidestep the issue by means of a referendum asking Canadians whether they wished to relieve the government from its pledge not to introduce conscription for overseas service. English Canadians by and large had said yes; French Canadians had said no. But because there had been no actual need for troops overseas the issue had faded. In the autumn of 1944 the matter stood differently.

Military men with few exceptions *knew* where *they* would obtain the replacements. In Canada there was a pool of trained men pressed into uniform under the National Resources Mobilization Act of 1940. They were officially known as NRMA men, to be used in home defence only. The soldiers who volunteered for General Service, and many other Canadians, contemptuously called the conscripts "zombies," the living dead. Why not send *them* overseas? From 1940 on attempts were made, usually accompanied by unsubtle peer pressure, to get them to opt for General Service, but the rate of success declined steadily. By October 1944 the Minister of National Defence, Colonel J.L. Ralston, had received enough military advice to persuade him that some of the NRMA men must be sent overseas. The issues, to him, were the adequate reinforcement and the morale of the fighting troops.

Unwilling to adopt a policy that had nearly torn the country apart in 1917 while it divided the Liberal Party, Mackenzie King turned to a new Minister of National Defence. Lieutenant-General A.G.L. McNaughton, who had until late in 1943 been

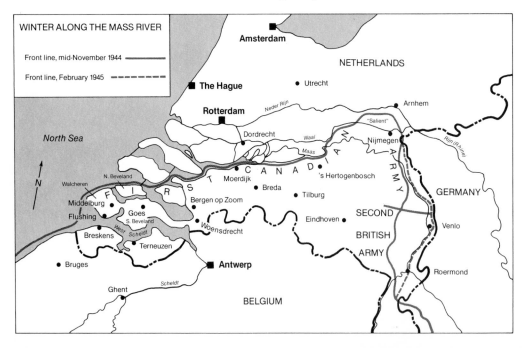

PUBLIC ARCHIVES CANADA, DND 42719 / F. DUBERVILLE

PUBLIC ARCHIVES CANADA, DND 43237 / M.M. DEAN

Although the Allied line of advance across the southern Netherlands was virtually static from November 1944 to early February 1945, there were frequent skirmishes with German troops. Civilians had to be evacuated from the area and some of them took their bicycles along with them on the backs of army vehicles.

Three members of the South Saskatchewan Regiment boil water in a helmet over an open fire. The winter months were unusually cold by Dutch standards and one of the soldiers' main preoccupations was keeping warm.

47

PUBLIC ARCHIVES CANADA, DND 43909 / G. AIKMAN

Sherman tanks of the British Columbia Regiment line up for a foray into German-held territory. Much of the activity during the winter months was aimed at probing enemy strength as well as keeping the Canadian troops active and alert.

The 5th Field Regiment of the Royal Canadian Artillery fire a twenty-five pounder in the snow.

PUBLIC ARCHIVES CANADA, DND 45745 / M.M. DEAN

commander-in-chief of the Canadian Army overseas, entered the cabinet at the beginning of November. He had committed himself to lead another attempt to recruit volunteers for General Service from among the NRMA men. It was an unprofitable enterprise. The English Canadian press was conscriptionist and critical of the government; French Canadian newspapers opposed conscription. Public opinion seems to have been less polarized than this would indicate, but the country was split along predictable lines. King's Cabinet was also split. When it became clear that the number of volunteers would be nowhere near enough, the Prime Minister, fearful as well of a revolt among his ministers, swung over to the conscriptionist side. One minister, Charles Power of Quebec City, resigned in protest, but the French Canadian ministers stuck with King. The crisis was over.

As estimates of manpower needs, based as they were on the experience of the recent past, turned out to be too high, few of the NRMA men ended up serving in Europe. Only 2,463 of them were actually posted to units of the First Canadian Army. Casualties in this group totalled almost 300. Of greater significance was that, although there was unhappiness among and mutual recrimination between the major ethnic groups in Canada, a government dedicated to their collaboration had survived. Canadians entered the winter of 1944-45 generally of one mind that the most important task facing them was the defeat of Germany.

To a Netherlander living in the still occupied northern part of his country the Canadian problem of national unity, had he known of it, would have seemed trivial. The failure of the Allies to complete the enemy's defeat in the West put the Netherlands in a perilous position. At the beginning of Operation "Market-Garden" the 30,000 railway workers, prompted by the Dutch government-in-exile, had gone out on strike in order to impede German supply lines. They did not return to work. Henceforth the only trains that ran were operated by German personnel and, with few exceptions, solely for military purposes. Because in the early aftermath of the strike all water transport was reserved for the use of the *Wehrmacht*, serious problems with the civilian

The Queen's Own Rifles in winter camouflage suits patrol the area around Nijmegen.

49

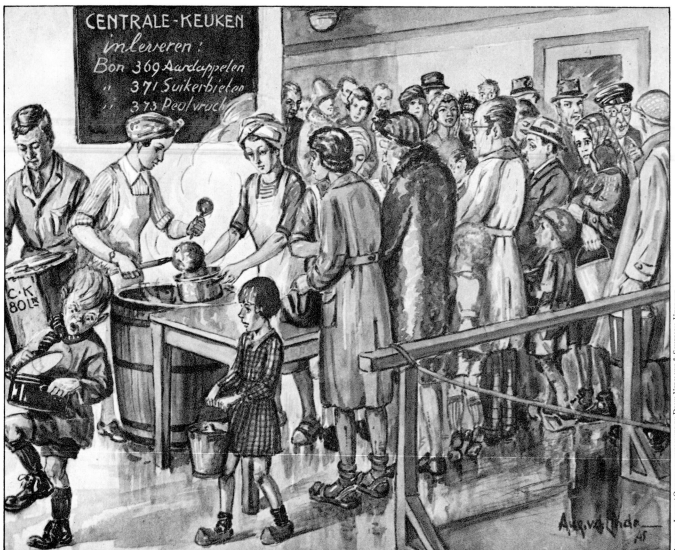

AUG. V.D. LINDE / ORIGINALLY PUBLISHED BY DRUK VERSLUYS & SCHERJON, UTRECHT

food supply arose almost immediately. This hardship was compounded by the German reluctance to ship coal from the Ruhr valley into the Netherlands—the Dutch mines had been captured by the Americans in mid-September—for any but the most pressing reasons. Supplying Dutch civilians with fuel or electricity was not one of them.

Even before September the Dutch diet was far from ample. Average daily caloric intake per adult had declined from an estimated 3,000 before the occupation to an official ration of just over half that in August 1944. Meat was virtually absent from the diet of Netherlanders, and the poor among them had been suffering from slow starvation for many months. They were being joined by ever more members of the urban skilled working and middle classes. The daily ration, consisting mainly of bread, potatoes and sugar beets, fell to 1,040 calories by November 1 and to half that in late January. It rose to 770 in March before falling again in April, to a low of 320 late in that month. Among civilians generally only farmers and those who had access to them and the wherewithal to barter with them got more than the ration. What all this meant becomes horribly obvious when it is noted that 2,400 to 3,000 calories constitute a

This illustration, painted by a Dutch artist in 1945, depicts a communal soup kitchen. In the cities of the western Netherlands during the winter of 1944-45, people of all social classes had to rely on communal resources to obtain adequate nourishment. The sign on the wall gives the cost in ration coupons of potatoes, sugar beets and green beans.

The "Hunger Winter" was hardest on those who began the war with the fewest economic resources. Poor people in the major urban areas were reduced to a diet based on sugar beets and flower bulbs.

normal daily intake for adult males, and 1,700 to 2,400 for non-pregnant females. With hard work the requirement increases, as it does in the case of pregnancy and lactation.

As for coal, it was almost the sole source of energy in the Netherlands at that time. Coal was used to generate electricity and produce gas. It was essential to the purification and pumping of drinking water, to the operation of the sewage system, and to the drainage of the polders. Several million Netherlanders lived below sea level; in late 1944 they were threatened simultaneously with death by starvation and by drowning.

First electricity was rationed; before the end of November it was no longer available to civilians. Gas was cut not long afterward. The authorities had more urgent needs for the coal: to maintain the supply of water and to keep the land from flooding, or at least that part of it that the Germans were not flooding for military purposes to defend themselves against the Allies.

The "Hunger Winter" of 1944-45: who, having lived through it, can forget it? All public transportation had ceased. People used dilapidated bicycles or walked. Underfed, they tired quickly either way. Food and fuel became the two great obsessions, the two substances that could still induce people to go long distances. But particularly in the cities and towns of "Randstad Holland," the conurbation which extends in a crescent from Dordrecht in the south through Rotterdam, Schiedam, Delft, The Hague, Leiden, Haarlem, Amsterdam, Hilversum and Amersfoort to Utrecht, food and fuel were ever harder to get hold of. In the flourishing black market, supplied by farmers, food was still available, but at prices only the wealthy could pay. It became common in this illicit and risky commerce for people to pay a hundred times the pre-war price for staples like flour and potatoes. Small wonder that the latter were boiled in the skin!

By unhappy coincidence it was a more than ordinarily cold winter. Many waterways froze up before the end of December and did not clear again until the beginning of February. This compounded the other difficulties. For several weeks ships and barges could not move food stocks, such as they were, from the north and east of the country to the more heavily populated west. The shortage of fuel was intensified by the cold, the ragged clothing worn by many the more inadequate because of it. Textiles and leather had been in short supply for years; and in the autumn the Germans had requisitioned clothing for the use of the troops on the Russian front. Everything seemed to conspire to make life harder for city dwellers.

From September on another tribulation beset the country. Eager to reduce the number of younger men in the Netherlands (this with an eye to the possibility of a resistance-led revolt coinciding with an Allied offensive) and to obtain workers for the construction of defensive positions and for the war industries in Germany, the Germans sought to round up as many young men as possible. Systematic raids (*razzias*) of entire neighbourhoods and towns yielded thousands of men between the ages of seventeen and forty. Other men hardly dared show themselves in public any more and went into hiding, unless they felt confident that their work in the Netherlands was regarded as essential.

The resistance (the main body was now referred to as the *Binnenlandse Strijdkrachten*—Internal Fighting Forces) was hampered in its various tasks. The *razzias* weakened it at a time when it faced unprecedented problems in gathering food for the thousands of hidden Jews and other *onderduikers*, wanted people of all kinds. There were debilitating quarrels about the sorts of political and social changes that might be necessary in the post-war Netherlands, and suspicions on the part of the more conservative elements of the motives of the Communists. Security had become a more serious problem than ever before (and it had always been deadly serious). Many recruits had joined the several resistance organizations in the late summer and early autumn; many veterans snidely called them "the knights of September." The newcomers were inexperienced and often careless, and more than ever carelessness cost lives.

The mood of the German police forces became increasingly vicious that autumn and winter. In part this may have been rage linked to the looming defeat of the Third Reich;

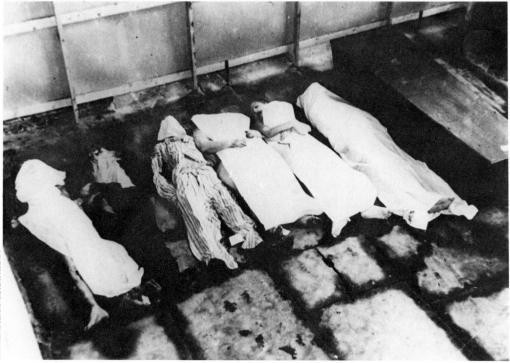

Municipal Archives, Amsterdam

Malnutrition contributed to the breakdown of public health, and the very young and very old suffered the highest casualty rate. Resources became so scarce during the last winter of the war that the dead could not be buried because of a lack of wood for coffins.

in part it was a reaction against the activities of some of the resistance groups. A number of unofficial, freelance groups had taken form, some of them bands of outright criminals. These murdered German soldiers and policemen, Dutch Nazis and collaborators, out of a mixture of motives: patriotism, private gain, even the sheer thrill of killing. Added to the activities of the mainline resistance groups, the operations of the irregulars enraged the enemy. Never loath to use terror, the Germans retaliated vigorously. Attacks against the agents of the German occupation were repaid tenfold.

Two of the more startling instances should be cited. An abortive attack in September on some German military equipment led to the deliberate burning of much of the nearby village of Putten and the eventual death in captivity of 552 of its male inhabitants. After the (unintended) wounding in March of the German police chief Hans Rauter more than 300 hostages, many of them leaders of the resistance, were summarily executed in reprisal. The figures tell the story: from May 1940 until the end of December 1944 a total of 1,228 Netherlanders were shot in reprisal for offences against Germans or Dutch Nazis and collaborators; from January 1, 1945, to the end of the war, no fewer than 1,579 hostages and even casual passers-by were executed. Not infrequently the shootings took place in public and the bodies were left where they fell as a warning.

Add to these horrors the occasional bombing of military targets, which generally exacted civilian victims as well, and a picture of hell on earth is nearly complete. Indeed, not just military objectives were bombed. On March 3, 1945, an error in navigation led a British squadron to unload its cargo of destruction on the Bezuidenhout residential quarter of The Hague. Several dozen civilians died and were injured.

As the weeks dragged on the prospects for survival dimmed. Although the Allied advance in northwest Europe resumed in February, the new offensive was directed away from the Netherlands, into the Rhineland. Starvation and disease claimed a mounting number of victims. The efforts of the public health authorities were undermined by a shortage of medicine and a collapse of normal standards of cleanliness as well as, of course, the grossly inadequate supply of food and fuel. Where the supply of drinking water could no longer be treated typhoid fever became a menace. Ever more people seen by medical personnel were lice-ridden. As rats were increasingly bold in

Dutch men were not to be seen on the streets during the last winter; they had either been sent to Germany for slave labour or they were in hiding. The gathering of food and fuel largely became the responsibility of women and children.

53

their foraging, this raised the spectre of a typhus epidemic. Numerous other diseases took more lives than they did in more normal times; weakened by malnutrition, the very young and the old died by thousands. And death brought with it a final indignity. "Even to be buried you have to queue up," a bitter joke went. There was a shortage of wood—as fuel it was precious—so it was replaced in coffins by cardboard. Then even that ran out. There was also a shortage of gravediggers. In one Amsterdam church in January 235 corpses lay waiting, name tags attached to the emaciated wrists. Eventually they were wrapped in sheets and buried in a mass grave. There was one recorded instance where a family in a one-room dwelling kept a corpse for five weeks in order to retain the ration coupons of the deceased woman.

Some people keeled over in the streets, faint with hunger, and died because no one was able to help them. Most continued the struggle. In the final months the hunt for food and fuel was carried on primarily by women and teenaged girls and boys, who could move about without fear of being grabbed for slave labour. From the towns and cities they headed into the countryside, pedalling patched-up bicycles—since rubber tires were virtually unobtainable, wooden strips were made to do instead—or pulling carts. Their hope was to be able to get, by barter or begging, grain, potatoes, sugar beets, anything edible at all. Some of the farming population dealt fairly with the hunger trekkers. Others took ruthless advantage of them. There was a real shift of wealth from town to country. Suspicious of the inflated paper currency, few farmers would accept it. They much preferred silver and gold, or furs and high-quality textiles.

Getting food was half the battle; getting it home again the other half. Criminals preyed on returning women; it was often easier to steal someone else's treasure than to

During the last winter of the war the Germans flooded areas of the Netherlands in an attempt to slow down the advance of Allied troops. This illustration by a Dutch artist depicts the flight of refugees displaced from their inundated lands.

AUG. V. D. LINDE / ORIGINALLY PUBLISHED BY DRUK VERSLUYS & SCHERJON, UTRECHT

find your own. In addition, men of the *Landwacht*, a collaborationist security force, became notorious for confiscating the food so painfully obtained. Indeed, a lot of crime came to revolve around food. By December bakers' carts in most cities had to be accompanied by armed policemen. Nevertheless attempts were made to steal bread from the carts; the constables guarding them shot first and asked questions later.

People also went to bizarre lengths to get fuel, mostly illegally and again at the risk of being shot. In many parks the trees were cut down, and ties were torn from streetcar tracks. Houses or buildings damaged by bombardment were visited by scavengers who stripped from them all the wood they could find. In many communities deserted buildings shared the same fate. In extremity people burned their own furniture or tore the woodwork out of their own homes in order to feed the small stoves on which they cooked their meager meals and around which they tried to keep warm.

Many schools stopped classes when the Christmas holidays began, so during the winter families huddled together. The economy ground to a virtual halt, except for those industries that the Germans deemed essential. Most people stayed home, in bed even, as much as they could, emerging only to go to the municipal soup kitchens for their portion of unappetizing liquid, or to scrounge for scraps of food and fuel. Recipes began to appear in the papers, themselves becoming steadily thinner, for fried tulip bulbs and onion and dahlia soup. Pet lovers tried to keep their animals, and succeeded surprisingly often, but cats and dogs were apt to be rustled and slaughtered.

A curfew kept Netherlanders from the streets at night, but there was in any case little for them to do. Most places of amusement closed during the winter; those that stayed open were generally aimed at a clientele which could afford the outlandish prices asked for food and liquor—wealthy collaborators and black marketeers. *They* were dancing on the edge of the volcano; most of their compatriots could only sit at home and wait for liberation, or death.

Many Netherlanders were bewildered by what was happening. Only those who had battery-operated radios—they were illegal, of course—could get news from abroad. No one really knew how much to believe of what appeared in the newspapers, legal and illegal. The rumour mill was the only civilian industry to be working overtime. People did know, however, that their situation was getting steadily more desperate. Occasional food shipments through the Swedish Red Cross could not disguise that basic fact. That conditions did not become more chaotic than they were owed something to the German military presence, but it owed more to the organization of Dutch life.

Occupying one of the most densely settled areas of the world, generally surrounded on all sides by people whom they may not like, may even mistrust and hate, yet cannot avoid or banish and must therefore accommodate, Netherlanders of necessity have for a long time lived in an unusually highly regulated society. Bureaucratic regulation and self-regulation combined in 1944-45 to prevent a disintegration of social life. There was much "looking out for number one" but also much cooperation and a general attempt to preserve as much of the normal code of behaviour as possible. Not least was this true of the civil service, and especially of those working in the embattled area of food distribution. Both publicly and privately there existed a strong impulse to deal with mounting disaster in an orderly fashion. After all, the liberation from the nightmare had to come some day, surely soon? As March turned into April and winter into spring one prayerful question was in the minds of millions: "Lord, how long?"

Soldiers unload Christmas mail for the troops in the Netherlands.

Canadian soldiers not only planned Christmas parties for Dutch children but also made toys to be handed out as presents.

Dutch children line up upon arrival for a party given by the Argyll and Sutherland Highlanders in Elshout.

The army commander, General Crerar, sits with St. Nicholas at a party at the Canadian army mess in Tilburg.

Canadian, British, and American soldiers organized a special party for Jewish children to celebrate the holiday of Chanukah.

The soldiers often gave the children food to take home for their families. At this party, the children were given loaves of white bread by an army baker just before they left.

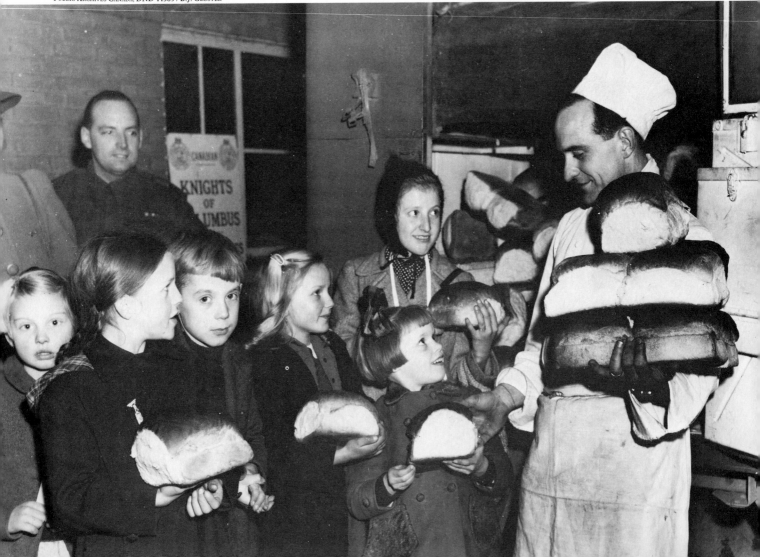

Johanna Foster & Maria Haayen

The Hunger Journey

Johanna Gertruida and Maria Hendrika, sisters in the family Van Santen, were young teenage girls living in The Hague when the war began. Like thousands of other people who lived in the western Netherlands, they remember their war experiences as a constant search for sustenance and warmth.

JOHANNA FOSTER: By the middle of 1943 the situation was getting very bad. We were beginning to starve. We hardly ever saw my mother, who spent her days in the surrounding farming areas trying to get food. She would be given a few potatoes at one farm, then trade some of them for vegetables at another, and bring home whatever she had at night. In the city, there were no cats or dogs to be seen in the streets, and it was quite common to find the head of a dog lying in the gutter. I was very proud and hated to ask strangers for food, but my mother had no such pride because she had children to look after. Due to malnutrition, my father contracted tuberculosis and was sent away to a sanatorium, so the rest of the family had to manage on its own for a long time.

MARIA HAAYEN: Every day was a fight for life. I remember going to look for wood, to a place that was being watched by a guard with a big dog. When he saw us, he told us to leave. I said to him: "If you let us in, I'll give you my bread ration coupon." But, when he agreed, I threatened to report him for taking a bribe, and then told him he would not get a thing from either me or my sister.

When you are hungry, all you ever do is dream about food. That was the most important thing in our conversations—dreaming about the time after the war when we could have cake, and eggnog, and chocolate, and rice with butter, and sugar. One time, I was looking through the house for something to eat and I found a small crust from the end of a piece of black bread. I went to bed early and hid the crust under my pillow. Lying in bed, I kept thinking about eating the crust, thinking so hard that I could almost taste it between my teeth. Then, suddenly, there was a terrific commotion, and my sisters came in shouting: "Where is the bread?" They had also had their eyes on it and we all had to share this small crust, less than a bite for each of us.

In the summer of 1943, we went to visit our

Maria Haayen (left) and Johanna Foster today. Johanna, the eldest sister, married an Englishman after the war, and Maria married a Dutchman. Both couples eventually settled in Guelph, Ontario.

DAVID KAUFMAN

father at the tuberculosis sanatorium in the eastern part of the country. While there, we befriended a farmer in the area who gave us some food to take home. Later on, when the food situation became desperate and there was almost nothing left to eat in the western Netherlands, I managed to get a railroad pass from the underground and made a trip east to see this farmer again. He and his friends gave me a lot of food as well as an old baby carriage in which to carry it home. Not only did I face a long walk back to the city, but I also had to outsmart Germans on the way who were intent on taking the food from me. The way home took me across a bridge on the IJssel River which was under German guard. I decided to hide my packages in the woods, and then walked across the bridge and told the guards I had not found anything on my trip. I then parked the empty carriage on the far bank, went down to the river, and swam back and forth under the bridge to get the food across.

After some time, I felt I couldn't continue on foot anymore. I was walking on wooden shoes, without proper clothing, and it was beginning to snow. I finally made it to the train station at Utrecht, where I managed to sneak onto a flat railway car in a train going to The Hague. I was helped up onto the train by a strange man who seemed to be in a state of shock from the war. But he was very sweet, and I got such a feeling of love from this man that I trusted him when he offered to guard my carriage, and I fell asleep beside him with his coat wrapped around me for warmth.

Eventually, I reached home with all the food. My two sisters were waiting for me. I was almost hysterical. I yelled at Johanna to make me some "power food"—a mixture of oatmeal and eggs. Then I fell asleep and did not get up again for thirty-six hours.

Rachel Stern

Dutch Jews: Years in Hiding

For reasons rooted in the history and social attitudes of the Netherlands, a large number of Dutch people took part in activities to protect Jews from the Nazis. In the early years of the war, mistreatment of the Jews provoked open defiance of the Nazis on the part of Dutch individuals and institutions, but of course, such defiance could not be sustained. One joke characterized the Dutch attitude thus: "Let those rotten Germans keep their rotten hands off our rotten Jews!" But it wasn't only their Jews that the Dutch protected; they also took in German Jewish refugees. Many of the Jews who survived the war in the Netherlands did so with the help of underground groups who provided them with hiding places or false identifications.

Rachel Stern (née Veffer) grew up in the town of Bussum, not far from Amsterdam. She, her parents, and five brothers spent the last three years of the war in hiding.

The Flower Shop

The year 1940 was comparatively uneventful except for the incident at my family's flower shop. We lived above the store, and I remember one morning there was a commotion outside. We looked out and saw a lot of people pointing at the store window. On it someone had painted a star of David and the word *Jood* in big letters. We were horrified. Later on we found out that it was a gang of Dutch Nazis who were responsible for the act. The intention was that no one should shop at

The family Veffer: Rachel, her parents, and her five brothers in a photograph taken before they went into hiding.

our store because we were Jewish, but instead the opposite occurred. That day the whole town came out and bought everything in our store, down to the last flowers and vase.

Star of David

One evening in 1941, our rabbi came to our home and said he had some things to tell us. He revealed that the Germans were appointing a Jewish committee in every city and town in the Netherlands, and that these committees were to tell us what we could or could not do from then on. He told us that we children could no longer go to school, and that no one in the family could attend public events such as sports matches, or go to public places such as movie houses. But the worst was to come: out of an envelope he pulled several stars of David made out of a yellow material, and he instructed us to sew them on every piece of clothing so that they would be clearly visible when we went out. We were now branded people, and when the Germans decided to round us up, it was to be easy for them to pick us out.

Grandfather's Funeral

When my grandfather died, my father decided to attend the funeral in Amsterdam. We could still travel but preferred not to because of the dangers facing Jews in public places. The next day we were eagerly awaiting my father's return. When he came back in the afternoon, he looked dreadful. He walked right past me without saying a word and sat down in the living room, trembling. My mother called the doctor, and an hour later, after he took a sedative, my father calmed down enough to tell us what had happened.

He had arrived in Amsterdam and attended the funeral without incident, but when he returned to the station to board the train home, he was accosted by two German soldiers. They stopped him, asked him what he was doing there, and when he replied, started yelling that he had no business being there and that he should have been in a concentration camp. A third German soldier came up and asked my father for his identification card. The card was clearly marked with a "J", for Jew, and also showed that my father's age was forty-one. Fortunately at that time the Germans were only deporting younger people, and the soldiers began to discuss this matter of my father's age. The conductor of the train, who had been watching all this, picked up my father's pipe which had fallen on the platform, handed it to him, and told him to board the train. As soon as my father got on, the conductor blew the whistle and the train left the station, bringing my father safely back to us.

Into Hiding

In 1942 the pressures became very great. The Germans were rounding up the Netherlands' Jews and sending them to the ghetto in Amsterdam from where they would be transported to concentration camps. Luckily for me and my brothers, my mother had no illusions about the camps; she knew that once we were sent there, we would be as good as dead. My parents decided we'd go into hiding. Of course, the question arose immediately: who would take in two adults and six children? But luckily for us again, the underground helped us find hiding places, the last one of which was a single room where we lived for three years.

I've always wondered about our fate in finding that particular room. It was in a house that was set slightly forward from the rest of the houses on the street. The room itself was upstairs on the second floor, and to our great

good fortune, not only had windows at the front facing the street but also had a side window. Together, these windows gave us a complete view of the street and advance warning in case of a raid by the Germans.

The room itself was only nine by twelve feet. It had a large bed against one wall where my parents slept, a small cot for me, and mattresses for my five brothers which we kept under the bed during the day. Near the front windows was a table with chairs. There was no running water, just a washstand and basin. Every morning, the people downstairs would bring us water. We had a screen behind which we would dress, and then it would be put out in the hall with a pail that would serve as our toilet. We cooked on a small wood stove. Most of the day there was no electricity, and when there was, it was used by the people downstairs for their cooking.

Usually our day would begin around noon, sometimes later, since my father believed that if we slept or stayed in bed, we would be less hungry. When we got up, we each had our daily chores. My brother Max was our lookout. He would go to the window immediately and peer out through a small hole in the curtain. My brother Joe would spend all his time lying on the bed, reading. He never left the bed and therefore developed terrible problems with his legs. I would try to clean up

The house in Bussum where the Veffer family hid in an upstairs room still stands today. The windows, three facing the front and one on the left side offering a view of the length of the street, remain unchanged.

the room. The stove burnt day and night, winter and summer, and the dust would settle so thickly that it was difficult to keep the room clean, but I did the best I could. My father had made a cupboard into a hiding place. In the event of a raid, it would have been impossible for the people downstairs to explain the presence of a family of eight, so a hiding place was necessary. Every now and then, my father would yell "Raid!" and we would all have to scramble into the cupboard with our belongings.

The Raid

One day my brother Max, at his usual spot at the window, yelled out: "Mom, Dad, come see what is happening. I think the Germans are here!" We all rushed over to the window and, sure enough, the trucks were blocking one end of the street and the Germans were coming towards our house from the other. This wasn't the usual raid called by my father; this was the real thing and we were scrambling for our lives. The man downstairs was home, and he came running upstairs and got us all into the cupboard, but we couldn't fit all our belongings in with us. We were in terror. My father had to put the burning stove outside, and then he grabbed me and two of my younger brothers and ran with us through the back yard to one of the neighbours. The neighbour looked startled when my father knocked on the door. My father said: "Don't ask questions. Just help me hide these children." The neighbour had a shed and in the middle of the shed floor was a pit. They lowered me and my brothers into it, covered it with planks, and then piled bags of cement weighing several hundred pounds on top. We were sitting with our knees touching our chins, and I had my arms around my brothers who were so little and frightened. The men yelled to us to be quiet and said they would be back as soon as the Germans had left.

Sitting there, we could barely breathe. The pit was so well sealed that I kept thinking that we were going to suffocate even before the Germans got to us. My brothers started to cry, but I told them to keep quiet and tried not to show how scared I was. Thank God, the Germans arrived. We heard their pounding on the door and their boots marching above

us. Of course, they saw nothing but an empty building with a bunch of cement bags piled right in the middle of the floor, and they walked right out.

I whispered to my brothers that they could rest easy, but the people outside, in their joy at the Germans' departure, forgot about us completely. I felt like we were suffocating and started to panic. I tried to hunch up with my shoulders and raise the bags of cement, but I couldn't move them. My head started to pound and I thought it would burst. I asked my brothers to help me, and somehow we finally managed to move the planks and tumble the cement all down and around us. When I look back at it now, I think we must have looked awfully funny, like three little ghosts. The noise from the falling cement attracted the attention of the adults. They apologized, and hugged and kissed us, but all

After the war, Rachel Veffer met Martin Stern, a soldier in the Lincoln and Welland Regiment. They were married in Bussum in April 1946 and settled in Toronto where they raised a family of five children.

DAVID KAUFMAN

I could think was that I wanted to see my mother and find out that everybody else was safe. It took us a week to get rid of all the dust and clear the cement from our lungs.

The Will to Live

One night in particular stands out very clearly in my mind, a night when we had been in hiding for two and a half years. Tensions were mounting, and the strain of confinement was beginning to show on all of us in the house. It was especially visible on my mother who was a very strong person. Her spirit was slowly breaking down. That particular day had been a very bad one, and after a terrible fight between her and the woman downstairs, my mother decided she would give us all up. She just said that anything would be better than what we were going through. If we were going to die, she thought it might as well be in the fresh air. She told us to get dressed and to pack up our belongings. It was late at night, and dark, and we just sat there like a bunch of ghosts, grey in appearance. There was silence, total silence. Daybreak came, and my mother, looking at us, changed her mind. She decided that, even if we were going to die, it was still worth making one more attempt to live in that room. We got undressed and back into bed, and stayed in hiding.

Wilhelmina Skinner

One Day at a Time

Wilhelmina Skinner (née Klaverdijk) was born in Rotterdam and was sixteen years old at the beginning of the war.

In the fall of 1944, my father was working for the Germans in the construction of bunkers on the coast. He had no other choice. My two older brothers—one was fifteen and the other seventeen—were picked up and shipped to slave labour camps in Germany. There had been a large roundup of all eligible men in Rotterdam; the only ones left were those who were already working for the Germans. People shared a common desperation and learned to live one day at a time. If you had food for a

day, you considered yourself very lucky and hoped to get some the next day again. Along with everything else, the Allies were carrying out nightly bombing raids in an attempt to destroy German U-boat bases, so we didn't get much sleep. There was no heat; it was cold and miserable. And the Germans stole all the bicycles and I had to walk to work every day more than an hour in each direction.

I was working in an office at the time. The money I made was not very useful, and, like many other people, I got involved in the black market. Most people weren't interested in money but in trading goods. You exchanged one item for another until you got what you wanted, which in my case was food. My family's apartment had been destroyed in the German bombing of Rotterdam at the start of the war, and consequently we had received special ration coupons for new clothing; only those people who had lost their posssessions in the bombing could receive the special permits. But there was little available in the shops for purchase and my mother wanted to discard the coupons. However, because my job was in the office of a small clothing manufacturer, I knew that the clothing could be obtained. Therefore, I took the coupons for the pyjamas and nightgowns to a certain lingerie shop and ordered the items for my family.

The proprietress at the shop was very pleased to take my order. She knew she could get merchandise with my permits, but she actually had no intention of turning the goods over to me since she could sell them on the black market at inflated prices. Of course the woman did not know that I myself was involved in the clothing business and, despite my young age, understood how clothing could be obtained even under wartime conditions. During a period of two months, I went back to the store many times and really got fed up. The proprietress kept trying to give me the brush-off. She kept telling me that the order had not arrived, but I knew she should have obtained the order by then. So one day I went in and told her that my boyfriend was getting impatient because I had to return to the shop so often. She asked me in a sarcastic voice what my boyfriend had to do with it. So I replied that my boyfriend happened to be in the Gestapo (which of course was not true) and that he would come into the shop with me on my next visit in order to speed things up. Well she nearly fainted, and a week later I had my pyjamas and nightgowns—all of excellent quality.

There was a man whom I knew who came to do business at the office where I worked and who was employed by the Germans. He worked with the security police and was involved in seizing food from civilians who had travelled to the country to trade their remaining valuables for farm produce. I knew he had the food I wanted and I told him about the clothing I had obtained. When he saw the clothes, he was impressed with their quality and offered to buy them from me. But I wasn't interested in money—I wanted food. He tried to deny that he could get anything, but I had seen what was going on in my office and knew that he had given food products to my boss in exchange for clothing—no money ever passed between them. I demanded a really outrageous amount of food. I was really desperate because my father had by this time developed hunger edema, could not get out of bed, and was in danger of dying. Anyway, this man knew that I was desperate and would do anything to get what I needed, so he finally gave me what I wanted—beans and peas, grains and fat, all kinds of food stuffs—and that saved my father's life. When I brought all the parcels home, my mother was terrified. She thought that I had been out with a German soldier. When I told her the story, how I had traded the coupons for clothing and the clothing for food, she and the other members of my family thought I had an awful lot of nerve for a young girl—which I did. In those days you had to have a lot of nerve or you didn't survive.

During that last winter, my younger brother, who was fourteen, would climb down into the basements of bombed-out buildings to find wood for heating fuel. The Germans didn't permit this, but my brother was young and very blonde and therefore could get away with things that adults couldn't do. He would even go to the German mess to beg for soup. My brother probably reminded the German soldiers of their own children at home. Wood was so scarce that many people dismantled the attic staircases within their homes. The most beautiful things were burnt for cooking and heating. We burnt all our books. We used a

Wilhelmina Skinner today.

little stove made from a juice can. There wasn't much to cook anyway. We ate lots of sugar beets and flower bulbs.

In the cities we had a curfew, and one time I was out too late. On my way home I had to cross a wooden bridge, so I took my shoes off in order not to make too much noise. But the wood creaked, a soldier at one end ordered me to halt, and when I didn't, he fired a shot that went past my feet. The soldier then approached me. He was carrying a lantern and I could see that he was no older than I was. He started to tell me that I had no business being out at that hour, but I decided to give him hell and told him he had a lot of nerve shooting at some innocent girl on her way home. I also bluffed and told him that his watch wasn't keeping time correctly, but it didn't matter what I said; he wasn't going to let me go. I realized that here was a soldier who wanted to do his job right, so I decided to fix him. I wasn't afraid—from one day to the next you didn't know if you would live or die. I said: "Okay. You keep me here, and my mother will be worried, but you will be even more worried." And he asked me why. "Because tomorrow," I said, "when your officer comes

65

here and you get off duty, I will tell him that you kept me here for your pleasure." Well, I was an attractive girl, and my threat scared the hell out of the guy. He let me go and I got home safely. That was the closest call I had.

After the war, Wilhelmina Klaverdijk met and married Howard Kenneth Skinner, a private in the signal corps of the 1st Division, and came to Canada in August 1946.

Vicki Tassie

Days of Awe

In these excerpts from her account of life in Holland under German occupation, Mrs. Tassie describes the hardships faced by the Dutch in the darkest days of the war's last winter.

The fuel problem was tackled in many ways. People trekked en masse into the country, going from farm to farm to find fuel of some kind. Others, armed with axes and knives, began to cut down trees, advertising signs and park benches. It was forbidden, so it had to be done after sunset. It became a familiar sound at night, the noise of cutting in the dark which stopped whenever German boots were heard approaching. When a tree came down, men and women would suddenly appear like vultures and throw themselves upon it, cutting branches off or simply tearing at it with their hands. In The Hague, all parks were de-treed. The cities, already bombed and scarred, became more desolate-looking every day. Housewives energetically hammered pieces of asphalt out of the roads; everything which could burn helped. The German commander of The Hague announced that anyone found cutting up a street would be shot without warning. The reaction to it was indifference: "So what else is new. . . ."

In November, bulletins were put up in store windows and on the streets requisitioning textile goods. Everybody had to hand in a certain amount in blankets and men's clothing because, as the posters said, "the German army needed them." We needed them too; with no heat in the houses and the stores empty, everyone needed whatever was left to keep warm, but that was of no importance. To hand them in meant helping the enemy, but the posters warned that there would be house-to-house checks for receipts, and if no receipts were shown the furniture would be seized. Some groups set to work forging receipts and that helped, but many people did not have the courage to take the risk, so the Nazis got their goods. The following Sunday in church our minister asked support for the needy in the congregation (their number was growing alarmingly) and added: "In the past week it has become clear that many of you still have things to give away"—a little pause—"even blankets. This time, it is not the enemy who *demands*, but the Lord of the Church who *asks*." Deadly silence, and people avoided looking at each other. . . .

On November 21, at 6 a.m., trucks appeared in the streets with loudspeakers blaring the order for men to report. Everyone between sixteen and forty had to stand in front of his door with an extra pair of shoes and food for two days; the women were ordered to stay indoors. District after district was cordoned off and soldiers were posted on both ends of the streets so that no one could get away. They collected the men that were standing outside and searched the houses where there were none out. Thirteen thousand men were caught, far fewer than in Rotterdam, partly because the soldiers searching the houses did not look too closely, in contrast with the political police that conducted the searches in Rotterdam. It just depended on who came to your door. . . .

Altogether, more than 120,000 Dutch men were sent to Germany for slave labour. Wherever they passed on their way to the border the population came to their aid. People gave whatever they could spare of their meager supplies: some apples, a pair of socks, a bit of milk, and hundreds of men were helped to escape. . . .

In the Christmas week our rations went down to three and a half pieces of bread and two potatoes a day. After butter and margarine, sugar had now disappeared too, and only children got a little bit of skim milk. We began to eat sugar beets and mixed them with the scarce potatoes to make the taste less obnoxious. We counted ourselves lucky when

Aug. v.d. Linde / Originally published by Druk Versluys & Scherjon, Utrecht

we could get salt on the black market (at twenty guilders a pound) to spice it a bit. . . .

The news did anything but live up to the tidings of Peace on Earth: the Nazis had started an offensive in the Ardennes and were making unexpected gains. Thoroughly depressed, we felt that they were determined to fight themselves to death, and that they were dragging us with them. . . .

Once Hans [a friend] gave me some potato coupons that had been destined for people in hiding. They had been caught and he was left with the coupons. I got two small bags of potatoes on them, and brought one to the van Kempens. They were an elderly couple, friends of my parents, that were in poor health and could not go food-hunting. It was the first time that I saw Mr. van Kempen, usually so

reserved, near tears. The other bag I gave to a family nearby with young children. It was more than welcome. Though extremely hard up, they had invited to Christmas dinner a family whose father had been shot, and so had used up all their reserves. And now, unexpectedly, some of it was replenished. Their joy was such that I knew they must have been desperate. When I walked home in the dark, having delivered my potatoes, I felt at peace as never before. It was a feeling that could only be expressed with the Shunnamite woman's: "It is well.". . .

The only distraction left, reading books or pre-war magazines, had its peculiar drawbacks. Leafing through a woman's magazine of 1938, my eye was struck by a notice: Important announcement. It turned

One of the ways the Dutch dealt with the fuel shortage was to cut down the trees on the streets. This contributed to the feeling of desolation in urban areas.

out to be an announcement about the coming Christmas issue. For one moment I was dumbfounded, then I burst out laughing and read it to my sister who looked unbelieving and reacted the same way. Did they really call such a thing "important"? Then there was a picture of a "terrible accident"—two cars had collided and several people were killed. We shook our heads, hardly believing our eyes. "Terrible," when the bodies could be claimed and buried decently—what a curious way of using words we had in those pre-war days.

Christmas Eve, 1944

Until the start of Operation "Veritable" on February 8, the winter of 1944-45 was a largely uneventful period for Canadian troops in the southern Netherlands. The time was passed mainly in patrolling and probing at the enemy lines. However, the soldiers never knew what to expect at the front; on any given day there could be surprises, and Christmas Eve, 1944, was no exception. Three former officers recall that not quite silent night.

J. Armand Ross (Régiment de la Chaudière)

On Christmas Eve we were very close to the Germans. There was no patrolling and we could hear that they were having a few drinks. At midnight they played Christmas carols over loudspeakers. I decided to respond with a few shots of mortar just to let them know that we were not friends. After the mortar fire they played "Lili Marlene" and then the music stopped. The men were homesick that night, but the morale was still good. All our men were, in fact, practising Catholics, so the padre went from trench to trench giving communion.

My company was also in line on New Year's Eve. One of the regiment's companies was needed to reinforce another regiment. We drew lots and I lost, so my company had to spend the second holiday in combat. During the night I went around the company and visited each trench. I had been given a bottle of scotch and I gave each man a small shot from my precious treasure. This was naturally much appreciated.

Ben Dunkelman (Queen's Own Rifles of Canada)

I remember Christmas 1944 very well. We were in the lines overlooking the Waal flats and Germany, and the Germans faced us in heavily defended positions. It being Christmas Eve, we were quite relaxed. The Germans started a Christmas party and we could hear girls' voices and singing; apparently they were having a lot of fun. My men found the mood contagious and thought that this was the real Christmas spirit, so they started to get out of their trenches, but I quickly ordered them back. However, just then, the Germans started to fire off all kinds of tracers; it was the most beautiful sight you've ever seen—much better than a fireworks display. And then, without warning, they brought down a heavy blanket of fire onto our position. Thank God the men were under cover. This was a great Christmas present from Hitler of Nazi Germany.

Joe Pigott (Royal Hamilton Light Infantry)

Towards the end of the war, around Christmas of 1944, we were south of Nijmegen, in a town called Groesbeek, literally face to face with the enemy across the street. I remember that Christmas Eve that year was very quiet both during the day and evening. In fact we could hear the Germans playing an accordion and singing. But close to midnight, when all was very quiet, one of the Canadian soldiers yelled out in a very loud voice: "Adolf Hitler is a son of a bitch!" For about thirty seconds there was dead silence, and then, from across the street came an answer: "And so's Mackenzie King!"

Chris Vokes

A Waste of Young Lives

Major-General Chris Vokes commanded the 1st Infantry Division in Italy and was transferred to the Netherlands in late November 1944 to the command of the 4th Armoured Division. Vokes, well liked but, in his own words, "sometimes too outspoken," had several run-ins with the army commander, General Crerar, over dress regulations. "I didn't care what a soldier wore as long as he could fight," Vokes says, but Crerar insisted that "the men had to go to battle with their gaiters and ties on." When Vokes was transferred to the Netherlands, Crerar told him that he wouldn't tolerate any of the slack habits adopted in Italy.

There were differences of opinion of greater consequence than arguments over dress. In January 1945, Vokes was ordered to engage in a local action of which he didn't approve and which ended up costing many Canadian lives.

In January, the 4th Armoured Division was ordered to make a third attempt to capture the barge harbour of Kapelsche Veer, on an island in the Lower Maas, north-east of Geertruidenberg. It was located on very flat terrain, and the weather was very cold. The only land approach to the harbour was along a dike that ran parallel to the river about three hundred yards from its edge. The initial effort to reduce the German position had been made by the 1st Polish Armoured Division at the end of December. A second attempt, by the 47th Royal Marine Commando, also failed, and then, for some reason, they wanted us to have a go at it. I was told to do it. As far as I was concerned, the Germans could have stayed there for the rest of the war. They were doing no harm. The position had been a bridgehead of sorts when the Germans still had visions of crossing the Maas and moving on Antwerp, but at this late date they couldn't have done any damage. I thought that the action was a great waste of young lives. But I had to do it—you can't just say no when an order comes down from army headquarters.

Chris Vokes, in retirement today (above), and as commanding officer of the 4th Armoured Division in the Netherlands in January 1945 (left).

Public Archives Canada, DND 45564 / D.I. Grant

Canadian soldiers trained for the assault on the German position at Kapelsche Veer by making practice runs in canoes, but the weather eventually proved to be too cold and prevented the successful completion of a water-borne operation.

It was bitterly cold, and the weather spoiled my effort to take the German position with a minimum of losses. When the action was first suggested to me, I said I would take it on, very reluctantly, if they could provide me with twenty-eight Peterborough canoes, because I had visions of sending the troops down the river in those silent craft under the cover of darkness. For a while I thought that by asking for the canoes, I might have turned the whole thing off. Well, it wasn't. The canoes were provided—flown in specially from Canada—and I had to go ahead. The soldiers practised in the canoes, but then we got a bitter cold spell, and the marshes along the banks of the river froze up. The canoe attack was attempted but movement was hampered by the ice and it failed. We had no choice then but to attack along the dike from both sides. The Germans had tunnelled into the dike, with their machine guns pointing out. You couldn't hit them with mortars and you had to take them from the flanks, which was pretty slow work. It took us four to five days to reduce the position, but by then, the Germans had gotten out. It cost us a lot of casualties. A lot of soldiers also got frostbite, but at least they came back alive.

John Spurr

Questions of Character

John Spurr, Chief Librarian Emeritus of Royal Military College, served as historical officer with the 4th Armoured Division. The historical officers' mandate was "to see as much as we could, learn as much as we could from direct interviews, and to report as much as we could to the historical office in London." Spurr was sent from England to the southern Netherlands in November 1944. In a recent interview, he made these observations about the Dutch and their German adversaries.

When I joined the division, our headquarters was in the town of Vught, which was a dormitory suburb of the city of 's Hertogenbosch. The town was upper-middle class and we had comfortable billets there. The inhabitants of the town, and indeed the whole province, were in very poor physical condition. When we went in, it was estimated that the average sustenance for the population was about eight hundred calories per day, which was below starvation level. Of course we rushed supplies in with all possible speed, and in about a month we had raised the daily caloric intake per person to twelve hundred, which was at least temporarily bearable.

Most people had contacts with a Canadian, and as our rations were supplemented by generous parcels from home, Dutch people were able to share our food. As a matter of fact, there was quite a competition to billet Canadians because the civilians knew they would get this benefit. Also, the civilians had no fuel aside from a certain amount of charcoal which could be obtained on the black market. I was able to bring nine pounds of coal a day into the house where I and several of my staff were billeted. It was a very cold winter in the Netherlands and this fuel was extremely welcome.

We all gained the impression of a people which had suffered greatly from almost every point of view. There had been a great deal of damage, not so much to homes in this province, but to public facilities such as transport and the vital water system. With almost no food and no social life, they were a people deprived, but they were a people of immense courage and steadfastness. Their devotion to the House of Orange was something that was always there. I remember, in the month of December, on the occasion of the birthday of one of the princesses, the whole town burst out into a rash of orange banners and flags. While Queen Wilhelmina was in England, and Princess Juliana in Canada, Prince Bernhard, who before the war had had the reputation of a European playboy, earned golden opinions from the Dutch because he kept up a constant liaison with his people, making frequent trips into the Netherlands at great risk to himself.

Dutch government officials were curiously helpless at that time because there was no transportation system, no communications

John Spurr.

PUBLIC ARCHIVES CANADA, DND 49078 / B.J. GLOSTER

system, no postal service or telegraph; they were almost entirely dependent on what we and the British could provide. Yet they kept everything orderly and cooperated with us to the limit of their ability. Regional feeings were very strong but nevertheless the people of the south had an enormous concern for their compatriots who were still under German occupation. Their hatred of the Germans was almost tangible; they weren't very demonstrative but it was in the air. If they did start to talk about it, the hatred would all pour out. They felt inadequate because, conditions being what they were, they could not help us very much in the military sense. But they were anxious to do anything they could for us, knowing that whatever they did would help in the liberation of their country, which was their goal.

Towards the end of the war, the Germans sent into battle both the very young and the very old. In some garrisons in islands off the southwest coast we found German battalions composed of men who were deaf, or of older men who had stomach ailments. It was also common to see boys of fifteen and sixteen in the POW camps. The young German soldiers were easily stirred by emotions and could be appropriately fanatical, but once they gave up, it was total surrender and they were really pathetic.

I spent interesting hours in the POW cages near the front lines, which in our territory would consist probably of a farmhouse with a large yard surrounded by barbed wire. The SS members would all be gathered in one section and the regular army prisoners in the rest of the yard—there was no love lost between the two groups. Many of the very young prisoners had been in the Hitler youth organizations and had been fed a lot of propaganda; they fully expected to be tortured and killed.

Later on, when we were in Germany, there was a point in time at which we were allowed to recruit non-Nazi prisoners who were

(Above and opposite) When the Canadians took prisoners during the last year of the war, it became apparent that the Germans were facing a severe manpower shortage. The captured prisoners included men as old as sixty and boys of fifteen and sixteen.

Public Archives Canada, DND 49075 / B.J. Gloster

willing to work with us in transport and other facilities. So one day I went over to a prisoner holding area and spotted a boy who seemed to be very intelligent and of reasonable physique, and I had him brought to me in the interrogation room. It was a bare room with a table and one chair on either side. I was sitting there smoking and tapping on the table with a riding crop which I carried out of habit—there was no intent of intimidation on my part. The boy stood rigidly at attention. I could see that his uniform had been thrown together from bits and pieces, and he was rather dirty, but he stood there, rigid and utterly defiant.

I asked him the standard questions—name, rank, etc.—and then a few more questions which he refused to answer. I could see that his lip was quivering a bit. Then he burst out in German, and though my German was very imperfect, I could understand what he was saying: "You can shoot me now. I won't say anything more!" He obviously knew some English, and in a mixture of languages, I asked him why he thought that I was going to shoot him. "Our officers told us," he replied. My interpreter came in and I told him to tell the lad to sit down, but the boy wouldn't move; so I barked the order at him in German and he sat down, trembling. I had a piece of chocolate in my pocket which I offered to him and which he refused to take the first time. However, when I offered a second time, he took the chocolate and also a cigarette. Then, through the interpreter I asked: "Now, when do you think we are going to shoot you?" I was smiling, and he looked at me and laughed suddenly. The tension was broken. He said: "I don't think you'll shoot me, sir. Maybe somebody else will. I don't think you will." Through the interpreter, I told him that nobody was going to shoot him, that he was perfectly safe, and that I wanted to know if he could drive a truck. Well, we had him enrolled in an auxiliary transport outfit and he did very well for us. A lot of them did.

The people of a small Dutch town watch the passage of 3rd Canadian Division troops on their liberation drive from the border of Germany in the south to the northeastern part of the Netherlands.

Chapter Three

The Liberation Campaign

For the First Canadian Army a relatively quiet three months ended on February 8, 1945. Operation "Veritable" commenced, the opening stage of the battle of the Rhineland. The chief objective was the Ruhr valley, Germany's most important industrial region, the site of many heavy industries essential to the Nazi war effort. In the weeks that followed, all the Allied armies on the western front advanced inexorably towards the Rhine, upstream from the Netherlands. That country was less important in Allied military planning than the Ruhr valley; it would have to wait weeks for liberation.

In the advance the Canadians again made up the left flank. The terrain was difficult. Along the Waal and Rhine the Germans had flooded the land; the wooded high country above the plain was well-defended. To the 2nd and 3rd Canadian divisions fell the unpleasant task of clearing the low-lying areas upstream from Nijmegen. This operation, uncomfortably reminiscent of the fighting along the Scheldt, was the first significant push of Canadian forces into Germany. But the area gained was modest, the personnel losses sizable. The war cemetery at Groesbeek, south of Nijmegen and just west of the Reichswald across the border in Germany, is a lasting memento of those losses.

The offensive resumed on February 22 with Operation "Blockbuster," in which the Canadians pushed further upstream towards the towns of Xanten and Wesel. Towards the end of the operation, by the first week of March, it became evident that the enemy was abandoning the left bank of the Rhine. Forward units of the First U.S. Army managed to capture a bridge across the Rhine at Remagen on March 7; two weeks later two further crossings were made, by the Third U.S. Army at Oppenheim south of Mainz, and by the Second British Army at Wesel. On March 25 all organized German resistance west of the Rhine had ceased.

While the 2nd Canadian Corps was struggling in the muddy and flooded fields along the Rhine, their comrades in the 1st Canadian Corps were preparing to join them. In February and March the 1st Infantry Division and 5th Armoured Division were moved from Italy to Belgium and the southern Netherlands. Soldiers found the contrast with Italy startling. "The people are willing to assist in any way within their powers," a transport officer wrote of the Dutch. "With these people, billeting has not been a difficult problem, in fact, they seem pleased to have you use their accommodation. . . ." On the night of April 1-2 the two Canadian Corps were united at last.

Two nights earlier the 8th Reconnaissance Regiment (14th Canadian Hussars) had crossed the border back into the Netherlands east of Arnhem. On April 1 units of the 5th Infantry Brigade liberated Doetinchem. The Canadians now fanned into the east and north. Much of the terrain was suitable to armoured warfare, and the industrial area of Twente was liberated by the 4th Armoured Division on April 4 and 5. Further west, the North Shore (N.B.) Regiment and Le Régiment de la Chaudière captured Zutphen

THE VICTORY CAMPAIGN—
SPRING OF 1945

Front line, Feb. 8, 1945 ⎯⎯⎯⎯⎯
Front line, Apr. 25, 1945 - - - - - - -

North Sea

N

Den Helder

Harlingen   16 Apr.   15 Apr. ●
15 Apr. ●   Leeuwarden   13-16 Apr.   Groningen   23 April-2 May
Delfzijl
3rd Cdn. Inf. Div.

18 Apr.   3rd
Cdn.
Inf.
Div.   Assen   7-8 Apr.
Airborne
(French &
Belgium)
Landings   1st
Pol.
Armd.
Div.   13 Apr.
10 Apr.

2nd
Cdn.

*IJsselmeer
(Zuider Zee)*

Haarlem

Amsterdam

Hilversum

Harderwijk   18 Apr.   1st Cdn.
Inf. Div.
5th
Cdn.
Armd.
Div.   16 Apr.

Barneveld   20 Apr.
49th (W.R.) Inf. Div.

Meppel   Inf.
Div.   1st
Pol.
Armd.
Div.   Coevorden
9 Apr.
4th
Cdn.
Armd.
Div.   Almelo
4 Apr.   Guards
Hengelo
2 Apr.

Zwolle
14 Apr.

Apeldoorn   13 Apr.   Deventer
12-13 Apr.

Zutphen

The Hague   Utrecht

Rotterdam

Neder. Rijn

Dordrecht

Kapelsche
Veer

26-30 Jan.

Breda

17 Apr.   Arnhem   2nd Cdn. Int. Div.
Doetinchem
1 Apr.

3 Apr.

Nijmegen   8-21 Feb.
1st Cdn. Army

's Hertogenbosch   Xanten   8 Mar.   Wesel
11 Mar.

Armd.
Div.

Armd.
Div.

*On February 8, 1945,
Canadian troops began their
push into Germany. Troops
had to be transported in
amphibious vehicles (below
and opposite) because of
widespread flooding caused by
the Germans around the area
of Nijmegen.*

76

on April 8, and two days later the Regina Rifles and the Royal Winnipeg Rifles entered Deventer. The Dutch *Binnenlandse Strijdkrachten*, the armed resistance, were given credit for helping to clear the city.

To the 1st Canadian Corps now fell the task of clearing the central and western Netherlands, whereas the north was assigned to the 2nd Corps. In the latter area drops of French and Belgian parachutists were made during the night of April 7-8 in the Groningen-Coevorden-Zwolle triangle. On the 9th contact was made with advancing units of the 4th Canadian Armoured and 1st Polish Armoured Divisions. Assen was liberated by the 4th Infantry Bigade on April 13; that same day troops of the 2nd Division joined a vicious three-day battle for the northern city of Groningen.

Zwolle, the capital of the province of Overijssel, fell to the Allies on April 14. The following day the 7th Reconnaissance Regiment (17th Duke of York Royal Canadian Hussars) reached Leeuwarden, only to find that the 1st Armoured Car Regiment (The Royal Canadian Dragoons) had beaten them to the Friesland capital. The Hussars pushed further north immediately, reaching the North Sea north of Dokkum later on the 15th. Harlingen was liberated by the Highland Light Infantry of Canada on the 16th; all Friesland had been cleared of Germans two days later. Everywhere the Canadians received a stormy welcome: flag-waving people lined the roads and screamed their thanks.

The German occupation troops in the Netherlands, some 125,000 of them, were now cut off from contact by land with Germany. At the same time, the urban population of the central and western provinces was now entirely cut off from supplies of coal and from most of the food-exporting areas. So far the Canadians had found little evidence of starvation. But this changed after they crossed the IJssel. That river, which ran north

LEST WE FORGET
THIS CANADIAN DEAD 1914 1945 IS GERMANY
DONT FRATERNIZE!
D79
ONYX ROUTE STARTS HE

The official attitude towards the German populace was markedly different from the attitude towards the Dutch. However, though the interaction with civilians in the Netherlands was extremely warm when compared with relations in Germany, Canadian soldiers did not treat German civilians with the coldness seemingly called for in official orders.

(Opposite above) Soldiers of Le Régiment de la Chaudière on the move from Nijmegen to the German town of Cleve.

(Opposite below) Soldiers of the 2nd Canadian Infantry Division survey the damage on a street in the German town of Xanten.

(Below) Dead cattle in a farmyard indicate the severity of battle in the Hochwald forest area inside Germany.

Public Archives Canada, DND 46277 / C. McDougall

Public Archives Canada, DND 47622 / Ken Bell

The North Nova Scotia Highlanders enter Zutphen under fire in the breakthrough to the northern Netherlands.

As the Canadians enter Zutphen, an old man and other refugees emerge from the surrounding countryside and trudge back to the city carrying their belongings.

Canadian army vehicles moving through the town of Holten.

Les Fusiliers Mont-Royal in house-to-house fighting during the liberation of Groningen in mid-April 1945.

PUBLIC ARCHIVES CANADA, DND 49974 / J.M. SMITH

German prisoners are escorted through a suburb of Arnhem.

from the Rhine at Arnhem to the IJsselmeer, proved no great hindrance. On April 11 the Princess Patricia's Canadian Light Infantry (PPCLI) and the Seaforth Highlanders of Canada used Buffalo amphibious vehicles to get across after the artillery had prepared for the assault. They wasted little time in expanding their bridgehead.

Consisting of the 1st Infantry Division, the 5th Armoured Division, and the English 49th (West Riding) Division, the 1st Canadian Corps now cleared the southern and western sections of the province of Gelderland. After crossing the IJssel near Arnhem, the English on April 13-14 liberated that city at last and then pushed westward. Further north, the 1st Canadian Brigade took Apeldoorn, site of Queen Wilhelmina's summer estate, on the 16th, while the 5th Armoured Division pushed swiftly northward from Arnhem through Barneveld to the IJsselmeer. On April 19 this division, its task completed, handed over its sector to the 1st Infantry Division and headed east towards Germany.

In some places the enemy still offered determined resistance, but many surrendered while others retreated behind the formidable defensive line focused on the Eem and Grebbe rivers. Along that line, on April 22, the 1st Canadian and 49th (W.R.) Divisions halted, and active operations virtually ceased. The welfare of the civilian population in the still-occupied areas was more important than territorial gain now that the war was clearly coming to an end. Only in the north did fighting on Dutch soil continue. A bitter struggle for the harbour town of Delfzijl began on April 23; not until May 1 was it finally taken.

By this time a dramatic change had taken place in the west. Operation "Faust," the relief of the civilian population by the Allies, had begun. It had been planned half a year earlier. As far back as October 8, 1944, Queen Wilhelmina had appealed to President Roosevelt asking that steps be taken to provide for the relief of her people as soon as the Netherlands should have been liberated. A plan was soon prepared by SHAEF (Supreme Headquarters Allied Expeditionary Force) which divided the country into four sections or relief target areas. The first of these, Section A, was south of the Waal and thus very largely in Allied hands by the second week of November. During the winter there was a refinement of the plan as it affected the three remaining sections. Sections C, east and north of the IJssel, and B1, west of the IJssel but east of the central city of Utrecht, were for the most part liberated during April. It was in B1 that Canadian troops first encountered significant evidence of starvation among the urban population, and here as in the eastern and northern cities the food distributed by the Canadians was more than welcome.

It was no secret that the situation was much more critical in the still-occupied provinces of North Holland, South Holland and Utrecht. This section, B2, contained the most heavily populated areas of the Netherlands as well as its largest cities. Here the shortages of food, fuel and medicines were greatest and most menacing. Most of the land lay below sea level moreover. The Germans had already inundated some of it to hamper the Allied advance; it was feared that they might breach more dikes. In any case, lack of fuel to power the great pumping stations placed the entire region in danger of gradual flooding.

Mass death by starvation or by drowning: these were catastrophes the Allies had to avert. Prodded by the Dutch government-in-exile, the military leadership sought to begin the relief of the population even before the war had ended and without capture of

A platoon of the South Saskatchewan Regiment is pinned down by enemy machine gun fire in a farmyard.

PUBLIC ARCHIVES CANADA, DND 49857 / D. GURAVITCH

Public Archives Canada, DND 50797 / D.I. Grant

Canadian army vehicles pass through the town of Winschoten in the northern Netherlands near the German border.

the area by force. A convincing argument against the latter option was that it would cost thousands of lives, civilian and military, and much physical damage to the country, at a time when the war was clearly drawing to a close. The knowledge that the official ration by April 21 was down to 400 grams (less than a pound!) of bread per adult per week also impelled the Allies to seek a deal with the Germans.

The *Reichskommissar* for the Netherlands, Arthur Seyss-Inquart, was not averse to some sort of deal. Indeed in late April secret feelers went out from the German as well as the Allied side. An important figure in the Nazi hierarchy, Seyss-Inquart was not alone in still hoping for a separate peace with the Western Allies which would enable Germany to face the Soviet armies, by this time besieging Berlin, with all her remaining strength. A deal with the Allies that would allow them to relieve the Dutch would certainly not hinder Seyss-Inquart's scheme.

Two secret meetings took place in late April at a schoolhouse in Achterveld, just inside the Canadian lines. At the second of these, on April 30, Seyss-Inquart attended in person and met Lieutenant-General W. Bedell Smith, General Eisenhower's Chief of Staff, Lieutenant-General Charles Foulkes, the commander of the 1st Canadian Corps, and Prince Bernhard of the Netherlands. Curious eye-witnesses in the PPCLI wondered whether a surrender was being negotiated. After all, since April 27 a ceasefire had been in effect in this theatre of operations. But the servicemen were wrong: what was at stake at Achterveld was the relief of Dutch civilians.

In fact the first food drops took place on April 29. Lancashires and Flying Fortresses flew at altitudes of only a few hundred metres, dropping containers of food instead of bombs. Thousands of people below waved and screamed with joy. More than one airman has said that these were the most satisfying runs of the war. Delivery of food, medicines and fuel by land and water began on May 2. Accompanied by German troops, Allied convoys delivered goods to specified locations. Because of the understandable feebleness of the Dutch distribution network, much of the supplies did not immediately go where they would have done most good. But there is no doubt that Operation "Faust" saved some people from death.

The early days of May were rumour-packed, the tension almost unbearable. Late in

the evening of May 1, German radio announced that Hitler had fallen in the defense of Berlin and that Admiral Karl Doenitz was the new head of state. This set off wild speculation. Hitler's personal testament made Seyss-Inquart the new Minister of Foreign Affairs; this also fed the rumour mills. The *Reichskommissar* left immediately by speedboat for the German port of Kiel and a meeting with Doenitz. It was still Seyss-Inquart's hope to make a separate peace with the West; that this too was in the cards was one of the rumours swirling around the country he had left behind. His intention to return to it was thwarted by North Sea storms on May 3 and 4, and by the Allied unwillingness to give him free passage over land. After five years of ruling the Netherlands, Seyss-Inquart was played out. On May 8, the day Nazi Germany capitulated, he flew into Twente airport in the eastern Netherlands, where Canadian soldiers took him prisoner. He was later condemned to death for war crimes and, with other Nazi leaders, hanged at Nuremberg.

A rumour that the German military commander in the Netherlands, General Johannes Blaskowitz, would surrender to the Resistance was abruptly negated on May 4. That day Field Marshall Montgomery, as commander of the 21st Army Group, accepted the surrender of all German forces in Northwest Germany, Denmark and the Netherlands. The capitulation would take effect at 8 a.m. double British summer time on May 5. Radio Brussels made the announcement at 8.35 p.m. on the 4th; London brought the news at 2 minutes to nine.

Many Netherlanders took to the streets in spite of the curfew which took effect at nine. The Dutch tricolour, red, white and blue, appeared in the windows of many homes after having been hidden for five years. In some communities the Germans tolerated such manifestations; in others they shot at flags or people. To many of the soldiers the celebrations seemed a provocation, but some of them at least must have seen them as a welcome sign that the war was at an end.

To the Canadian troops the announcement came as an anticlimax. Most felt relief rather than exultation. According to C.P. Stacey, "the units' diaries make it clear that there were no cheers and few outward signs of emotion." On that evening General H.D.G. Crerar addressed a message to all ranks:

Friendly relations between soldiers and civilians in the Netherlands were encouraged. One of the surest methods of initiating an exchange was to offer a Dutch civilian a cigarette, and in this respect Canadian soldiers were always generous.

In the last days of April 1945, a compromise was struck between the Allies and the German administration in the occupied Netherlands to enable the starving populace to be fed. The details were worked out at meetings in a schoolhouse in the town of Achterveld (above). This resulted in food being transported by Canadian troops to points in no-man's land where it was picked up for distribution by Dutch personnel (left). This occurred about a full week before the liberation and helped save thousands from death by starvation.

From Sicily to the river Senio, from the beaches of Dieppe to those of Normandy and from thence through northern France, Belgium, Holland and north-west Germany, the Canadians and their Allied comrades in this army have carried out their responsibilities in the high traditions which they inherited. The official order that offensive operations of all troops of First Cdn Army will cease forthwith and that all fire will cease from 0800 hours tomorrow Saturday 5 May has been issued. Crushing and complete victory over the German enemy has been secured. In rejoicing at this supreme accomplishment we shall remember the friends who have paid the full price for the belief they also held that no sacrifice in the interests of the principles for which we fought could be too great.

The casualties of the First Canadian Army since the crossing of the Rhine on March 24 totalled 6,298, of which 1,482 were fatal. Total Canadian casualties in northwest Europe were almost 45,000, more than 11,000 of them fatal. In addition, United Kingdom, Polish, American, Belgian, Czechoslovak and Dutch units serving under Canadian command suffered more than 23,000 casualties, more than 4,000 of them fatal. By way of comparison, no fewer than 230,000 Netherlanders died as a result of the war. Jews, 104,000 of whom were murdered by the Nazis, made up the largest proportion of that number. Approximately 66,000 people died of the deprivations which came with war, 18,000 of starvation in the final winter alone.

Of the 9,200,000 Netherlanders who survived the war more than half waited nervously, eagerly, impatiently on the morning of May 5 for their first sight of Allied soldiers. In the meantime a power vacuum seemed to exist. "Seemed," because where the *Binnenlandse Strijdkrachten*, the armed resistance, took to the streets, conflict with the Germans soon followed. There were a number of deaths on May 5 from gunfire—eight in the city of Utrecht.

On that day General Blaskowitz met General Foulkes at a hotel in Wageningen to receive the terms of capitulation; Prince Bernhard also attended. It was agreed that on May 7 the 1st Canadian Corps would enter "Fortress Holland." With a view to preventing further difficulties, Blaskowitz exacted a promise that the resistance would be ordered not to carry arms until further notice. Prince Bernhard and Foulkes agreed that would be best. The following day Blaskowitz came again to sign the terms of capitulation. The stage was set for the triumphant Canadian entry into the great Dutch cities.

There the atmosphere was growing more tense by the hour. People could not understand why, the war apparently at an end, they were still under German control. On May 7 thousands trekked to the main roads, hoping to see the Canadians, but these were still waiting along the Grebbe line, sorting out problems with German officers. The 49th (w.r.) Division did move, but it liberated only the Amersfoort-Hilversum-Utrecht area and went no further west. Further deaths occurred: twenty-two in Amsterdam when the resistance and a German patrol exchanged shots on the Dam square.

May 8, V-E Day, was a day to remember. The sun shone brilliantly as the Canadian columns moved towards Amsterdam, Rotterdam, The Hague and the other cities and towns of the two provinces of Holland. They were greeted with a wild, desperate enthusiasm. These hundreds of thousands who stood along the road or broke across it to

PUBLIC ARCHIVES CANADA, DND 50470 / B. GILROY

The bands of the Royal Canadian Regiment and the 48th Highlanders of Canada parade through Apeldoorn in mid-April 1945.

Wherever the convoys appeared, crowds of people would gather to greet the liberating Canadians.

PUBLIC ARCHIVES CANADA, DND 50221 / D.I. GRANT

engulf the Canadian vehicles had seen death approach, and now saw it recede. The welcome to the soldiers who had helped to banish the spectre was bound to be near-hysterical. But there was more to it than that. After five years the miasma of oppression was lifted, the Nazi nightmare brought to an end. Never mind that hunger persisted, that many did not turn up to welcome their liberators because they were too weak to move from their houses, that the country had been ruined and robbed of much of its wealth; the horror was past. Liberation!

The Dutch euphoria was, in fact and in one word, unforgettable. We have many witnesses. Farley Mowat, an officer in the Hastings and Prince Edward Regiment: "The Dutch are a staid race, but when they broke loose, they simply flung off all restraint and went berserk." Captain T.J. Allen, the historical officer of 1st Division: "Whatever their routes, the convoys were greeted with the wildest enthusiasm by hysterically happy crowds. . . ." An officer with the 1st Canadian Transport Company, RCASC, charged with carrying the Seaforth Highlanders to Amsterdam: "It is impossible to describe the scene. . . . In retrospect it appears to be fantastic, but yet it happened. The enthusiasm that the peoples of Canada showed to their Majesties the King and Queen on their tour of Canada [1939] was as nothing compared to the reception the people of Amsterdam gave to us." John Morgan Gray, an intelligence officer: "The war might have been all futile madness but this seemed to me a splendid moment, if only for the excitement and the joy and the tears of the people beside the road." Captain Allen again: "Thousands . . . lined the roads and blocked the way through the towns, to laugh, to shout, to weep. To a liberated Dutchman that day it was a privilege even to touch the sleeve of a Canadian uniform. Each Canadian private was a Christ, a saviour. . . ." Exaggeration, no doubt, but pardonable given what happened on that once-in-a-lifetime day.

The exuberant celebration for a moment masked a darker reality. But the head of the SHAEF mission sent into the Netherlands soon reported about the B2 area: "The people, especially those in the big towns, are exhausted both physically and mentally. Generally speaking, they suffer from great weakness and the men are quite unable to perform a full day's work. It is reliably estimated that certainly fifty percent of the population are lousy. . . . It is of interest to note that there were five times as many males suffering from starvation as females." (The most likely explanation is that because women had become the main food gatherers they needed more energy and therefore got to eat more.) Brigadier W.B. Wedd, a civil affairs officer with the First Canadian Army, reported that a state of "acute general starvation" had been avoided by only two to three weeks. "Reports would indicate that death from starvation has been confined to the very old, the very young and the very poor." Rotterdam was worst off, but there were cases of acute starvation in all of the cities and towns of the two Hollands and the province of Utrecht.

The most pressing problem facing the 1st Canadian Corps in the early days of liberation, then, was civilian relief. Until the middle of May the Corps was responsible for the distribution of food and fuel in the B2 area. Public health also required attention. Canadian medical staff had to deal with menaces like typhus, typhoid fever and dysentery. DDT was used liberally, even with abandon, in the battle against lice, as Canadian personnel worked in cooperation with Dutch medical teams.

A problem almost as pressing as civilian relief, and one which required at least as much attention, was the German presence. The enemy, some 120,000 strong, had to be concentrated and disarmed, their equipment and supplies gathered together. This tricky enterprise, called operation "Eclipse," could not be done overnight. The Germans remained for some time under their own military discipline, and for several days after May 8 many units retained their arms. This confused many Netherlanders. "Some could not understand, during the first few days, a situation where armed soldiers were going up one side of the road and armed Germans going down the other side, neither interfering with the other," one officer wrote. "We had to deal simultaneously with a numerically superior German Army, with the Dutch Underground and with civilian matters." This was far from easy.

The Canadians feared that the resistance would seek to revenge themselves on Germans, Dutch Nazis, and collaborators. But the *Binnenlandse Strijdkrachten* took orders well, and there was surprisingly little trouble. Captain Allen approvingly cited one report: "Full credit is due all our crew that there were no incidents during a job involving fully armed and large German forces, a large civilian population, hungry and excited, a numerous underground armed and eager to help deal with the Germans." Operation "Eclipse" was indeed a success. Before the end of May the disarmed Germans were marching back to Germany via the northern route.

Yet there were untoward incidents in the first days of liberation. Not a few Canadians complained about the Dutch treatment of alleged Dutch Nazis and collaborators. One popular pastime was to shave the heads of women who were said to have consorted with Germans; the next step was often to paint the women's heads orange. Various other humiliations were inflicted on those who were believed to have misbehaved themselves during the occupation. Deliberate injury and even murder were not unknown. As well, the property of Nazis and collaborators was looted in more than one city.

This was lynch law, and mistakes *were* made. The eagerness of many Netherlanders to take revenge for five years of oppression, perhaps also to make amends for their own quiescence in the face of that oppression, prompted actions that could not be condoned. They can be understood, however: there was an intense and natural resentment against *landverraders*, traitors. Possibly the most demoralizing aspect of the occupation had been the evidence that some of one's compatriots sympathized with the enemy, helped him, joined his side. Now they must pay. The euphoria of liberation left room for the desire to strike back. It is quite conceivable that the Canadian and English soldiers stood in the way of greater excesses than actually took place.

If some Canadians were momentarily dismayed by Dutch vengefulness, they probably got over it quickly. To them, the heroes of liberation, the Netherlanders showed little but gratitude. The men of the 1st Division, and of the other divisions that were moved into the Netherlands during May, were idolized and feted. The experience was heady. The country might be poor and the people a bit the worse for wear, but who could resist that warmth, that love? And the war in Europe was over! The dangers of war behind them, the dull duties of civilian life ahead, they were ready for a bit of fun. While they waited for repatriation they set out, each in his own way, to make the most of their sojourn in the Netherlands.

Public Archives Canada, DND 49136 / M.M. Dean

The liberation was not only a time of joy but also a time of revenge. The pent-up anger of the populace was finally released and brought to bear against collaborators of all stripes. Those who had assisted the enemy were rounded up and paraded through the streets, and women who had consorted with German soldiers were publicly humiliated by having their heads shaven.

Public Archives Canada, DND 49753 / D.I. Grant

In Almelo a crowd forced a woman whose head had been shaven to stop and pose for a Canadian army photographer.

(Opposite) Dutch children came out to greet the Canadians as they passed through the cities and towns on the drive north and west during the month of April.

(Preceding pages) The town of Rijssen was taken without a fight by the Fort Garry Horse and Le Régiment de Maisonneuve. The townspeople, in expectation of their liberators, had spent the morning decorating the buildings with flags.

People celebrate in the streets of Dalfsen.

*Canadian soldiers parade
through the streets of
Harderwijk with Dutch girls
on their arms and other
civilians in tow.*

(Top) Members of the
Seaforth Highlanders of
Canada who had served in
Italy and participated in the
liberation of the Netherlands
express their eagerness to go
home.

(Above) Soldiers of the Lake
Superior Regiment display a
trophy of war.

A column of German prisoners is marched back from the front.

A German prisoner, one of two hundred taken after a failed attempt to recapture the town of Otterloo from the 5th Canadian Armoured Division.

Lt.-Gen. Charles Foulkes (left), commander of the 1st Canadian Corps, confers with Prince Bernhard just before dictating the surrender terms to the Germans on May 5 at Wageningen.

Seyss-Inquart, Reichskommissar of the Netherlands, (centre of the photograph) was placed under arrest by Canadian officers and escorted from the airport at Hengelo to First Canadian Army headquarters on May 8, 1945.

Ben Dunkelman

Almost without a Shot

In the final weeks of the war, Canadian 3rd Division troops crossed from Germany back into the Netherlands and pushed north past Zutphen and Deventer, all the way to Leeuwarden and on to the North Sea. Wherever possible, the Canadians tried to take population centres without a battle so as to spare the civilians from death or injury and to prevent damage to the towns and cities. One such effort that was successful took place at Pingjum in the northern province of Friesland.

In the northern Netherlands we entered an entirely different type of battle than the one fought in Germany, one more similar to our experience during the breakthrough in Normandy. We were formed into relatively small but powerful groups, and my company was given three tanks, several pieces of heavy artillery, machine guns, and heavy mortars. We were ordered north to clean up many pockets of resistance that remained. There really wasn't that much fighting, and it was a great experience. We liberated dozens of towns where the inhabitants would come to greet us and make banquets for us and bake cakes. Our biggest problem was trying to leave these wonderful people and continue on with the job we had to do. Eventually we reached the causeway across the Zuider Zee [IJsselmeer]. There we were told of a large German force entrenched to the north in the town of Pingjum, and we immediately headed off in that direction.

When we reached the crossroads a quarter of a mile in front of the town, we stopped and deployed our vehicles off the road. I met with the Dutch underground leader for the area who advised me that the troops in the town were fanatical Nazis led by a Green Shirt ss (a Green Shirt was an ss officer who trained troops). The Dutchman suggested that I contact the German commander and convince him to surrender. We went into a farmhouse at the crossroads, and, to my amazement, the Dutch leader was able to get the German commander on the phone. I had quite a talk

with him and we agreed that his men would surrender under my full protection as prisoners of war. He also said he would contact me within three hours to advise me of the timing of the surrender.

Several hours went by without contact. I had the Dutch underground leader call him again, and we had quite a conversation. The German commander told me he was having a little difficulty with his own subordinates but that he would contact me shortly. I waited another two hours—still no surrender. Dusk was fast approaching and I was becoming skeptical as to the German's intentions. I didn't want to engage in a set-piece battle in the town as I knew there would be many civilian casualties. He knew this as well and was literally holding the civilians hostage against me. I finally went into the farmhouse, set up my headquarters there, and I can recall staring at the map all night trying to work out a plan. We contacted the German commander several times again, but he still wouldn't set a deadline.

I decided that this situation couldn't go on forever. I found out from the Dutch underground that the town's northern sector wasn't heavily defended. I devised a plan in which part of our company would detour about twenty-five miles around Pingjum and enter it from the north side; then I ordered John Hancock, one of my commanders, to take the three tanks and other heavy support weapons and move north. I estimated that it would take him about three hours to get in position. Then I phoned the German commander and gave him an ultimatum, telling him that if he didn't surrender within two hours, I would attack the town and hold him responsible for any casualties.

Two hours later, John Hancock reported that he was in position, so our group attacked the town from the south to distract the Germans and then I ordered John into the assault. When he got into the town, John—six feet four inches with shoulders like a barn—jumped out of his jeep and ran down the street, shouting in German for the enemy to surrender and threatening them with dire consequences if they didn't. The Germans surrendered, and we didn't have to open heavy fire on the town and its civilians. For this action John was awarded the Military Cross.

John & Dieuwke Martens

Short and Tall

John Martens and his wife, Dieuwke, were both born in the northern province of Friesland. During the war, Mr. Martens was unable to continue his university studies and moved back north to his grandparents' home in a town not far from the village where his wife-to-be was living. They met during the war, eventually married, and came to Canada. Here they recall scenes from the liberation of Friesland which took place in mid-April 1945.

MRS. MARTENS: In mid-April we heard that the Canadians were in Sneek, only twenty kilometres distance from our village. My sister and I couldn't wait any longer, so we got on our bicycles with the wooden tires and drove in the direction of the soldiers. We first met a few Canadians walking along the side of the road carrying walkie-talkies, but a little further on we saw Germans in trucks, and still further on, we met Canadians again—it was chaos. But the Canadians were so good to look at—brown and happy—and of course we were exuberant. At first we thought they were British and called them "Tommies" which made them angry, but we couldn't speak English and they couldn't speak Dutch. The chaos lasted about a day. In the town we found some Canadian soldiers resting and handing out chocolate. I hadn't seen chocolate for years—just the idea of eating it was great.

MR. MARTENS: My uncle was a local commander of the Dutch internal forces. On the night before the liberation, he told me to take white paint and an axe and to go out during the night to paint over or destroy German road signs so as to confuse the retreating soldiers. I did it, but not very happily because I was in danger of getting shot by German guard detachments; in fact, two or three men were killed that night, and I don't think the action was very effective anyway.

The next morning it was very quiet. Buses passed through our village carrying Germans who looked rather haggard. I decided to ride out of the village on my bicycle. Several miles away, at a crossroads, I met a single Canadian soldier in a jeep who was looking through

binoculars. I was desperate for information and, after saying hello, asked him for a newspaper. He didn't have one but he gave me a pocketbook on which was written a short message from his girlfriend. I could see that his name was Roy and that he was from New Brunswick—I'll never forget that. He must have been a scout because the nearest troops were seven miles away. But I thought: *here was the liberator.* I went back to my village and that night a column of Canadians passed through. I remember seeing one soldier lying on top of the gun barrel of a tank; I could never understand how he did that.

What struck me when I watched the Canadians parade through the towns was the disparity in their statures as they marched. They were mixed up in their ranks—short guys and tall guys together. In contrast, the Germans were very orderly—all arranged by height. You would see great, tall Canadians marching beside little ones—it was very funny.

John and Dieuwke Martens today.

The day after the liberation of Workum, the town held all sorts of sports events, including a soccer game. One Canadian set off a string of fireworks and accidentally burned a hole in a girl's coat. I went over to talk to the soldier and said: "Don't worry. Fortunately nobody was killed." He burst out laughing. My English wasn't as good as I thought, for I had meant to say that nobody was hurt. The Canadians made immediate restitution for any damage, and the local commander made sure that the girl got payment for the cost of a new coat.

I remember one day seeing a column of about a hundred German prisoners of war marching under the escort of a half dozen Canadian soldiers and three or four members of the Dutch underground. One rough-looking German removed a long dagger from his tunic and handed it over to a Canadian. It was clear that he would not surrender it to one of the Dutchmen. The German soldiers were very proud and thought it beneath their dignity to be escorted by members of the underground, by fighters who didn't even wear uniforms.

MRS. MARTENS: After the liberation, the underground rounded up collaborators and forced them to stand at the edge of a canal with their hands in the air and their backs to the water. The collaborators had to stand straight, and if they dropped their hands, the underground members would fire over their heads to scare them. They didn't really harm them; it was just a way of taking a little bit of revenge.

In our village, there was only one girl who had gone with a German. She was arrested and her hair was cut short—she had beautiful black hair—and then she was placed under house arrest. She was kept inside until the celebrations after the liberation of the whole country. The people of our village decided they wouldn't participate unless she was free to do so as well. I also felt sorry for her. She had come from a poor family and had had to go to work at the age of fourteen. I think she was just looking for company and some affection. During the celebrations she was released, and people eventually forgave her and forgot about the matter.

Colin Friesen

A Better Cargo

Operation "Faust," the Allied food drop and convoy in the last days of the war, saved thousands of people who were on the brink of starvation in the most populated area of the Netherlands. Colin Friesen, now Bursar of Massey College in the University of Toronto, was then a pilot officer in No. 150 Squadron of British Bomber Command. He recalls that his flights for Operation "Faust" were far preferable to the twenty-four bombing missions that he flew earlier over France and Germany.

The first food drop mission I flew was on April 29 and took us over The Hague. Part of the area over which we were flying was still occupied by the Germans, so specific instructions from them, about the operation, were issued to us through our Bomber Command: we had to fly at a certain altitude, we had to remain strictly on course, and we could not signal anyone on the ground by tipping our wings. As the missions went on, we saw that every barn over which we flew had painted on its roof the words "Thank-you, Canadians!" We found this very touching because, up till then, we were people involved only in a process of destruction. Our second food drop was just a day later, also over The Hague, and by that time word must have spread that we were coming because we could see hosts of people gathered on the ground, and from the one thousand foot

Colin Friesen.

Aug. v.d. Linde / Originally published by Druk Versluys & Scherjon, Utrecht

altitude at which we were flying, we almost felt that we could hear their shouts of welcome. Our third mission, on May 1, took us to Rotterdam; the fourth one was to Gouda; and the fifth one was over Rotterdam again, on the day before the armistice was signed.

When you are in a theatre of war, you forget your own inward emotions. You have no idea of fear despite the fact that, in retrospect, it's like going to the gallows every day. I recall so vividly many of our operations: the wake-up call at two o'clock in the morning, then the drive to the dining hall for breakfast, and the table talk which was usually nothing more than bickering over who would have the extra bacon. Can you imagine—knowing that you may be going to the gallows and worrying about an extra piece of bacon?

When we flew over the occupied part of Holland, I was so relieved that I myself no longer had to be destructive, that I was not too concerned about the possibility of being fired upon by the German ground installations. I remember watching the German ack-ack guns and I can recall them following our progress, making absolutely sure that we obeyed the terms and conditions of the operation. The Germans were told our precise course and air speed and we had to let them know our position at various times during the flights. And then the Dutch people would appear everywhere in the vicinity of the drop—on treetops, on rooftops, everywhere waving banners and caps—and I'm sure of it, you felt you could hear them cheering.

Allied food drops brought relief to the starving population of the central Netherlands.

Vicki Tassie

The Snare
Is Broken

In this final excerpt from her account of the occupation, Mrs. Tassie describes the religious emotion with which the people of Holland greeted their day of delivery.

On Sunday, April 29, at about 1.30 p.m., we heard the roaring of planes. For a while now no bombing attacks had taken place and we wondered whether it was starting again. They came over low, and suddenly we realized: they have come with food. We ran up to the roof and everywhere people appeared—in the streets, on the roofs, hanging out of windows, waving with handkerchiefs, sheets and tablecloths, whatever they could get their hands on, to welcome the planes. It was a jubilating crowd, some people with the tears streaming down their cheeks, trying to speak and not able to articulate sounds because of their strong emotions. One has to have lived through that hunger winter to know the overpowering relief of seeing those food bombers, planes that for once were bringing life. The gratefulness was so intense that it dispersed all other feelings, and many a prayer of thanks were said that night.

Even though the food could not be distributed for some days, the moral effect was tremendous. That hundreds of bombers could fly above the cities in spite of the *Reichskommissar's* refusal was a miracle. [The general population was unaware at the time that these flights had been agreed to by the Germans.—Ed.] And the next days they came back, the "flying grocers," dropping millions of kilograms of food into fields where officials of the Bureau for Distribution of Food in Wartime stood ready to receive it and make an inventory.

With new hope, we listened to the BBC in our radio hide-outs. The news was more encouraging every day; on May 1 Hitler committed suicide, on May 2 Berlin surrendered, the Allies and the Russians had met in Germany. . . .

On Friday, May 4, we had listened as usual to the news with some friends and I was just ready to leave when Frits, who had been there earlier, suddenly appeared again. We were amazed to see him at curfew time. He looked from one to the other and said with wonderment: "They say that the war is over." We could not believe it but went back to the radio and Koos nervously started to turn knobs until he got the end of a broadcast. We did not know what had been said, but we heard a magnificent rendition of God Save the King and then the Marseillaise—and that could mean only one thing: victory. . . .

What can one do at such a moment? Our reactions were not those of Mad Tuesday any more—too much had happened since then. There was no thought of celebrating, we just felt that it was good to be together and that we wanted to share the joyful news with others. Light-headed from weakness and near tears, we kissed and shook hands, saying only each other's name. . . .

The next morning we heard that the surrender of the German army would be officially signed on Sunday afternoon and then our liberation would be a fact. Here and there flags started to appear, our own red, white and blue waving freely for the first time in five years. Boys and girls went arm in arm through the streets. The Noordeinde, the avenue where the Queen's palace stands, was teeming with people wearing orange ribbons, while trucks with German soldiers, rifles at

Cheering children greet an Allied food drop.

Citizens of The Hague read the first bulletins announcing the liberation.

The underground press is sold above ground. The sign says: "What was once underground is now legal."

German soldiers leave The Hague on foot.

their feet, roared through every once in a while.

It was a strange day in which we seemed to move as in a dream. Queen Wilhelmina addressed the country in a radio broadcast in these words:

Men and women of the Netherlands! Our language does not have words to express what lives in our hearts in this hour of the liberation of all Holland. Finally we are master in our own house again. The enemy has been driven from every corner of the country; gone is the execution squad, the prison and the torture camp. Gone is the nameless pressure of the persecutor who had tortured you for five years; gone is the terror of starvation. . . .

On Sunday, the occupation ended officially. All houses had flags out now, fugitives came out of hiding, and we could not stop repeating to each other that it was over! Strangers embraced and shook hands on the street. There were tears of joy, and immense and deep-felt gratitude, because on this beautiful

May day we had received that most precious gift: our freedom.

Church bells were pealing all over the country and people filled the churches for thanksgiving services. Our church was overcrowded, and I noticed friends and acquaintances that I had not seen for a long time, out in the daylight at last. . . . We heard a sermon based on the words spoken to Moses at the burning bush: "Put off your shoes from your feet, for the place on which you are standing is holy ground." Looking at people's faces I thought that these past five years had indeed been a confrontation with the Holy; many were so overcome with emotion that they could not join in the thanksgiving hymn "Now thank we all our God." A chord of genuine response was struck to the words of the 124th Psalm read in that service:

Blessed be the Lord, who has not given us as prey to their teeth!
We have escaped as a bird from the snare of the fowlers;
The snare is broken, and we have escaped!

DAVID KAUFMAN

Because of her underground experience, Vicki Hoeksma was asked after the war to assist Canadian intelligence personnel in identifying enemy agents and collaborators. At the border crossing where she was sent, she met an officer named James Tassie with whom she worked every day. They became engaged in October 1945 and were married about a month later.

T.J. Allen

Not With Triumph or Pity

The German surrender went into effect on the morning of May 5. At four o'clock in the afternoon, in the town of Wageningen, the 1st Canadian Corps commander, Lieutenant-General Charles Foulkes, met the 25th German Army commander, Colonel-General Johannes Blaskowitz, to dictate the terms of surrender. The scene was described in this report prepared by Captain T.J. Allen, historical officer with the First Division:

The meeting took place in a partially damaged, bare, and small hotel, "The World." Long tables had been set out in the lobby with chairs on one side for the Canadian staff officers and on the other side for the German staff officers. The remainder of the room was crowded with chairs for press photographers, movie cameramen, war correspondents and a variety of official onlookers. These chairs were rapidly filled. The first senior officer to arrive was Prince Bernhard of the Netherlands. Then came the Canadian staff officers followed immediately into the room by the Germans. The onlookers began to rise to their feet as Lieutenant-General Foulkes entered; he waved them back to their seats. Thus the Germans could have

General Foulkes (left) dictates the terms of surrender to General Blaskowitz (centre right).

no delusion that Canadian officers were standing respectfully for German generals. As soon as both German and Canadian officials had sat down, Lieutenant-General Foulkes, in clear and measured tones delivered the terms to the grey-haired, thin-lipped Colonel-General Blaskowitz, Commander of the 25th German Army. First came the general terms following a 21st Army Group instrument of surrender, then terms applying more specifically to the enemy troops in western Holland. "You are personally responsible to me for the discipline and maintenance of all German troops in western Holland. . . . You will provide a detailed order of battle. . . . You will provide me the plans for field demolitions, for routes, the signals layout, the codes. . . . You will have no communication with any other German formation. . . . You will disarm all your personnel when ordered by me and will dump all war material, when ordered. . . ." Thus the surrender was made explicit. One interesting turn of phrase was the following: "You will arrest immediately all persons connected with concentration camps except the inmates." So clause followed upon clause, Lieutenant-General Foulkes reading out each in English and pausing for the German interpreter to translate. General Blaskowitz would ask questions, these were translated into English by Lieutenant-General Foulkes' interpreter, but General Foulkes made it clear that he would allow no discussion of the terms, only questions regarding clarification or amplification. There was no pomp attendant upon this meeting of victor and vanquished, and only such modern circumstances as the clattering whirr of movie cameras and the harsh unnatural glare of floodlights. The Canadian voices were not triumphant but they held no pity. This German general incarnated the fate of the German might which now had no force, of the German will which now had no volition. Inexorably the German doom was upon its people: "You will . . . You must. . . ." For a brief moment the atmosphere of that shabby room of "The World" was charged with cosmic significance, and despair and hope exacted a full look at each other across a wooden table.

Bob Stier

The Last Casualties

Bob Stier enlisted in 1942 and served with the Saskatoon Light Infantry (M.G.) in Italy before arriving in the Netherlands.

In March 1945, our regiment and others that had come up from Italy congregated in the area of the Reichswald in Germany near the Dutch border and got set up to go back into battle in the final push up through the

Bob Stier met his wife-to-be, Betty, in Rotterdam. They were engaged in August 1945 and got married three months later.

Netherlands. In April, we went through Arnhem, then into Apeldoorn, through Nijkerk, and ended up just outside Amersfoort. We were a machine gun battalion travelling on Bren gun carriers and moving quickly all the time in order to keep up with the retreating Germans. A lot of the firing was only with machine guns and light artillery in keeping with the request of the Dutch government that civilian injury and damage to towns be kept to a minimum.

The day of the ceasefire was the strangest day. We had all our machine guns set up and then an order came through for us to stand by—no firing allowed. When the ceasefire was announced, everybody unloaded their guns. That night was terrible. It was too quiet. You were so used to sleeping with shells landing all about you and machine gun fire that when it became quiet that night, nobody could fall asleep.

Of course, you were glad to see the war over because you knew at least that you were going to get home in one piece. Even just a few days before the end, there was a platoon officer killed in our regiment. We had been sent out on a reconnaissance patrol to try to locate a retreating German unit. The officer was in front of the carrier, and I was just behind him. He stood up and got it right through the head. I had to lift his body off the front of the carrier so the driver could regain control of the vehicle. That was the last battle casualty in our company.

At the end of the war, we were stationed outside Amersfoort in a large camp. When it was known that the ceasefire would be coming, all our rum rations were saved up to celebrate the end of the war. The rum was mixed with Carnation milk to make enough to go around. Well, our company commander's batman got so plastered drinking this liquid that he fell asleep face down in his pillow, and we found him suffocated the next morning. It was an awful shock to find him like that. Some victory celebration that was!

A Grand and Glorious Transport Detail

On May 8, Canadian troops entered Amsterdam. A transport company officer filed this report on what he called "the most momentous hour any of us had ever spent."

First Canadian Corps Transport Company started on its journey to the liberation of one of the world's great cities. The instructions for the route were to follow Red route. However, after the convoy had proceeded for a few miles, the provosts were passed who were in the process of putting up the route signs. However, there was no difficulty with the route. . . . We passed several German troops inside German camps. They were still armed and apparently allowed to move about at leisure. An odd sight, to see a German soldier in uniform, fully armed, and to do nothing about it. The job of the various Canadian infantry regiments moving up today is to arrange for the collection of these Germans, to collect their arms and equipment, and to start them on their long journey back to Germany. Germans refuse to disarm until they have Allied guards as they are afraid that the Dutch people might start a policy of retaliation for the harm they have suffered during the five long years of occupation. . . . On the way up the people lined the streets and cheered us and waved to us as we passed. This welcome grew more intense as we drew closer to Amsterdam and as we entered just recently liberated areas. The welcome given us reached its climax as we entered Amsterdam. . . .

It is impossible to describe the scene . . . in retrospect it appears to be fantastic, but yet it happened. The enthusiasm that the peoples of Canada showed to their Majesties the King and Queen on their tour of Canada was as nothing compared to the reception the people of Amsterdam gave to us. Thousands of people were lined on the streets as we drove through, and to employ a figure of speech, they were wild with joy. All the buildings had flags and banners draped on them. The people were carrying flowers, flags, and streamers.

The drive through the city was made at a very slow rate, and each driver was handed large bouquets of flowers and flags were stuck onto the lorries. As the lorries entered the city there was a small bridge followed by a sharp turn which necessitated each lorry slowing down to almost a stop. At this point, the people started to climb onto the vehicles. Naturally because of the danger to life, the lack of military discipline, the danger of damage to the lorries, every effort was made to stop this practice. The civilian police, the boy scouts were out doing traffic control, the provost, the drivers themselves, and all the dispatch riders both of the infantry and Service Corps, all tried to stop this practice, but without avail. . . . Some stood, some sat, others just hung on wherever they could, in fact most hung on where one would think they couldn't hang on. There were on and in each ten tonner approximately one hundred and twenty-five people, and on each smaller vehicle a proportionately smaller number. Even the dispatch riders were forced to put up with three or four people hanging on to their machines. And so the convoy moved through the streets of Amsterdam, with thousands of people lining the streets and singing and cheering.

As the troops of the 1st Canadian Infantry Division moved into the western Netherlands starting on May 7, they were greeted with wild enthusiasm by an expectant and grateful population.

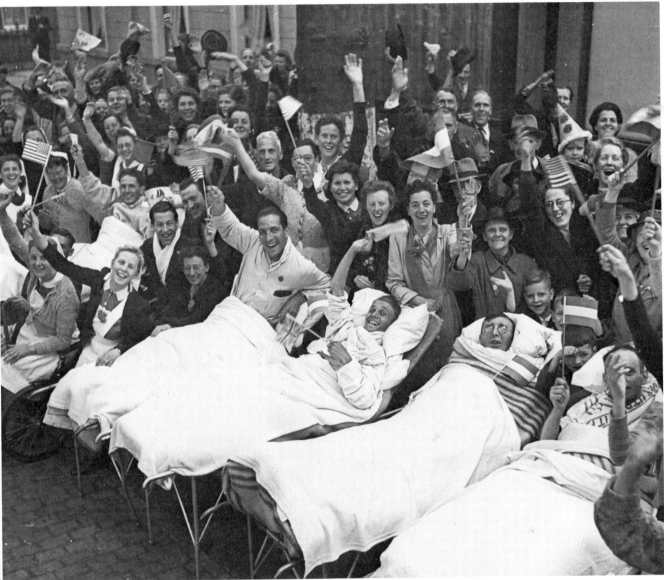

In Utrecht even the hospital patients were wheeled out onto the streets to greet the liberators.

Boys climb aboard an army truck in Rotterdam.

Flag wavers on a balcony in Utrecht.

(Opposite) Dutch girls join a convoy in Utrecht.

(Below) The welcoming crowds at Rotterdam.

*A tulip-bedecked army vehicle
is mobbed in Rotterdam.*

PUBLIC ARCHIVES CANADA, DND 52134 / M.M. DEAN

Johanna Foster & Maria Haayen

Saints and Sinners

The positive effect of the liberation on the Dutch perception of Canadians, a people the Dutch had not known at all before, was profound, but even after the liberation, when the Canadians stood in a plainer light, they still found favour in Dutch eyes, despite their foibles.

JOHANNA FOSTER: On the day that the war was over, we heard shouting in the streets. We got hold of a flag and went walking among the crowds. On a narrow street, some Germans started shooting. We fell flat on our faces and weren't hurt, but others were killed. Then we had to wait a few days until the Canadians arrived. Every day we went out with a basket of lilacs. I wore my father's shoes.

MARIA HAAYEN: I remember standing there, looking down the road which they would use to enter The Hague. On the third day, I saw a tank in the distance, with one soldier's head above it, and the blood drained out of my body, and I thought: *Here comes liberation.* And as the tank came nearer and nearer, I had no breath left, and the soldier stood up, and he was like a saint. There was a big hush over all the people, and it was suddenly broken by a big scream, as if it was out of the earth. And the people climbed on the tank, and took the soldier out, and they were crying. And we were running with the tanks and the jeeps, all the way into the city.

A group of civilians and soldiers pose beside a sign at Amsterdam indicating that the city had been liberated after almost exactly five years of occupation.

JOHANNA FOSTER: When the tanks came into the city, we ran all through the streets. And when the soldiers came out, if people had any food they offered some of it to them. We took chalk and wrote all over the streets, "Welcome liberators!" There was an explosion of emotions. The people went after the collaborators and loaded them onto carts like animals, and girls who had gone with Germans had their heads shaved.

The first extra food we got was biscuits. We lived near a canal and across it there was a little bakery shop. We would lie in front of the window of our house watching the shop for a sign that it was open, and when we saw it open, we raced across with our ration tickets. We got these beautiful little biscuits; they were dry but they contained whale oil and were made especially for people who had vitamin deficiencies. They tasted fabulous. Every person got a whole tin of the biscuits and could eat as much as he or she wanted.

In the days after the liberation there was a lot of music and dancing in the street. At first we didn't see too many Canadians because they were still settling into their barracks. My sister and I met our first Canadians about a week after the liberation, when we were sitting in a little restaurant with some of our girlfriends. A whole bunch of soldiers came in and one guy asked me to dance with him. I didn't want to because he was short, but he wouldn't take no for an answer. We thought that their manners were rough. One soldier came up and started going through all the girls, saying: "No, I don't want that one, no, not that one . . ." until he found someone that he liked. The girls had to wait to be picked by a soldier. I thought that was terrible. The Canadians treated us differently than the Dutch boys we had known, but nevertheless, they were our liberators.

We made friends with two of the Canadians and invited them to our house. I had told one of them that our younger sister was sick, and when he came over, he showed up with a jacket full of food for her. He was a very nice man. The Canadians didn't have the manners that Dutch men had at that time, but there was something innocent, something sweet about them. They were very nice.

DAVID KAUFMAN

Michiel Horn

Joyful Noises

Michiel Horn teaches history at Glendon College, York University, in Toronto. He was born in the town of Baarn, near Hilversum, and was nearly six years old when the Netherlands was liberated.

In April 1945 we heared that the "Tommies" were coming closer. A neighbour told us that the Canadians were moving against the German defensive positions in our area and that there was a possibility of shelling. My father had been physically reinforcing the cellar for this eventuality, and the next thing I knew, we were all down there—my four brothers and I, my parents, our maid, and a friend and her two children. I don't recall being frightened. The shelling sounded like fireworks—an ever-louder whistle, then *wham*—it was rather exciting. I remember some heavy firing with the occasional loud crash, but in due time it ended.

The following day the shelling was over. The Canadians had been aiming at a German battery a few hundred yards away; the house next door had received a direct hit on the roof, and the house opposite had been struck on the front porch, but except for a few knicks our house was undamaged. I found this all terribly impressive. My bothers and I wanted to go out into the garden, but we weren't allowed to do so because our parents feared that we might cut ourselves on shrapnel. A cousin of ours showed up and *he* was allowed to gather up shrapnel because he was older; we thought that was terribly unfair.

There was a quiet period at the very end of April and the beginning of May. Then one morning we were told that we were going to see the "Tommies." It was a very sunny day. We had to walk about a mile. There were a large number of people standing by the roadside and eventually we saw soldiers in trucks and half-tracks, and tanks approaching. People were deliriously happy, and we shared in the general excitement which was tremendous. The noise of the heavy vehicles,

particularly the tanks, was unbelievable, and we found it rather frightening. Then we went home. Later that day, a small column of troops parked along our street, and my parents and our neighbours went out to talk with the soldiers. I do recall that people were smoking, and I picked up an empty cigarette package with a picture of the bearded face of a sailor on it. We tore branches from the flowering shrubs in our garden and decorated the military vehicles with them; that was also exciting and we took great pride in the job we had done.

The English soldiers—I now know they were from the 49th (West Riding) Division—stayed in our town for about ten days and were then replaced by Canadians. I have no recollection of the Canadians being different from the "Tommies"; they were all the same to me. As time went on, there was more to eat. The first time I ate chocolate, I was violently ill, but I quickly got to like the taste. I remember little of that summer, except for the celebration of the Queen's birthday in August. People made festive arches of wood and flowers to hang around the town. Some of the arches even had light bulbs in them which were turned on for a limited period; I remember going out one evening to admire this sight.

That summer and fall, we saw a lot of Dutch flags in the town and heard patriotic songs for the first time; we could connect

Dutch children watch with fascination as soldiers repair a heavy vehicle.

these things with the arrival of the Canadians. In September I went to school, to grade one, and one of our first projects was learning about Canada. We found out that Canada had a lot of snow, and Eskimos and Indians, and wide-open spaces. Gradually, the Canadians left, and the excitement petered out. The tanks especially, after we got used to the noise, had been quite exciting, and we were disappointed to see them go.

Tillie Sugarman

Your Real Name

Mrs. Tillie Sugarman (née Bueno de Mesquita) was born in Amsterdam of Sephardic Jewish parents who had lived in the Netherlands for many generations. During the war, Mrs. Sugarman and other members of her family managed to obtain false papers and survived in the open by successfully concealing their true personal identities.

It was on May 4 that we knew for certain that the Germans were finally leaving for good. That night we sneaked out after curfew to visit friends; we were so angry that the Germans still had the nerve to be present and to try to prevent us from moving about freely. A few days later, the Canadians entered the city and everybody went out to greet them. Thousands of people lined the streets and crowded into Dam Square. The Canadians looked so brawny and healthy. Some of the people, out of generosity and gratitude, gave the liberating soldiers sugar beet cookies; it was supposed to be a treat for them, but I think it must have made some of the Canadians sick.

One of the first things the Canadians did was to go to the central kitchens and really spice up the soup we were fed, which was normally made with sugar beets and potato peelings. The next time we got the soup, it was fantastic—it had meat and vegetables and rice in it. And everybody who was suffering from hunger edema got extra rations almost immediately. When we went to pick up my

mother, she was very badly off and could hardly walk, but after three weeks with the extra food, she recovered very quickly and was running up and down stairs like a young girl. It was a period in which our feelings were all mixed—it was happy and sad. Not too many people came back from the concentration camps, and their relatives would go to check lists of survivors. I lost one of my brothers. So it was not an undiluted joy; you lost people as you gained freedom.

One of the most fantastic things was to go out on the streets under your own name, to say "this is my real name" and then actually say it. When you met people you had worked with in the underground, people you knew well, you would ask them who they really were—it was very exciting. But when you met other Jews, you didn't dare ask about their families, because it was likely that they had been killed; if their families had survived, you would be told about it. During the days of liberation, the weather was beautiful, and for the first time in five years I had time to look at the trees. I could really see that it was spring.

Intelligence: The Good from the Bad

When the Canadians entered the western Netherlands, one of their first concerns was the apprehension and arrest of known and suspected enemy agents and war criminals. This task fell to the counterintelligence units whose work is described here in two brief accounts. The first is by Lieutenant-Colonel William Tenhaaf (Ret.) who, at the time of the liberation, became second-in-command to the Area Security Officer for South Holland. The second account is by a former sergeant (who wishes to remain anonymous) who was a member of a twelve-man field security section also operating in the area of Rotterdam.

William Tenhaaf
On May 8, 1945, we drove into Rotterdam to set up our office. On arrival, we met with representatives of the Dutch underground and

liberation groups. What struck me about the city was the great gap at its centre which was the result of the bombing in 1940. We also saw that the population was emaciated. As we drove along the streets, older people would start crossing and walk right into the side of our vehicle; this behaviour was apparently the result of impaired vision and hearing caused by vitamin deficiencies. People were staggering in the streets, especially the elderly.

There was an air of revenge in Rotterdam, and our task was to seize people we wanted before they themselves could go underground. We had arrest categories which included certain ranks of the German ss, German police groups, etc. In Germany, this included judges, *landesrats*, and other officials. All these categories were identified and listed in a handbook issued by 21st Army Group for the occupation phase, Operation "Eclipse."

The persons belonging to the arrest categories were rounded up, arrested and taken to the appropriate camp or jail for identification, and either held for further questioning or cleared. In contrast to the normal process of arresting known agents, I didn't like this procedure very much because few of the people we picked up were guilty of a specific crime. However, this process had to be followed to make sure that we captured the people we were really after. If we found any Dutch collaborators, they were turned over to the Dutch authorities. In these activities, we were following policies laid down in consultations between the Dutch and British governments in London.

In the first three weeks, we managed to get about a hundred thousand German soldiers out of the Netherlands and back into Germany. At each prisoner sorting point, the faces of soldiers were scanned by a small group of Dutch underground members who could recognize enemy agents, collaborators and others who had served German intelligence. If the German soldier passed through this control point, he was home free and could go on to a demobilization camp in his own country; if not, he was placed under arrest. Of course, not all those dressed in German uniforms were soldiers; some were Dutchmen trying to escape their own country.

Our interrogation teams could handle as many as dozens of people per day, but it took

DAVID KAUFMAN

until September to interrogate all the people arrested in our security area. There were categories of people who had been arrested for the general reason that they were known, as a group, to be very loyal to the Nazi party, such as customs inspectors and clerks, but the only people we held eventually were those wanted either by the Dutch or some other government for war crimes.

Lt.-Col. William Tenhaaf (Ret.).

Sergeant, Security Section

In May 1945 we went to Apeldoorn to regroup and organize for the liberation of the western Netherlands. Each intelligence section was assigned an area, and we got Rotterdam. We had heard that the first jeep into Amsterdam was machine-gunned and therefore weren't sure if the Germans knew that the war was over. However, the reception we got in Rotterdam was just fantastic. We had a jeep leading our little convoy, followed by a large truck and a few other vehicles. As we drove through the crowds, people held up babies for us to touch and pieces of cardboard for us to autograph. We also saw people dropping on the street from starvation. We

Members of the Dutch underground round up Dutch Nazis and collaborators in Amsterdam.

Members of the underground were quick to set up their own interrogation procedures for suspected collaborators. Part of the job of Canadian intelligence units was to make sure that these interrogations did not get out of hand and that wanted persons were handed over to the proper authorities.

eventually got to the city hall where there was quite a greeting for us. You can never forget it.

In Rotterdam, we had seven targets to look after. The first one was a large barracks complete with Germans who were armed to the teeth. When we saw this place, we said to hell with it and asked the Dutch to give us a place to hang our hats. In the meantime, the trouble was that there were supposed to be Canadian troops coming up behind us for support, but nobody turned up for a few days, and initially we were on our own. Another of the hazards was the Dutch who were carrying weapons that had been dropped to them during the war. They were having a field day with those things.

After we got our headquarters set up we started to work with the Dutch underground and began filling up one of the jails with people we were looking for and had found. There was one guy we got in touch with who was known as Johnny the Killer. He had been an agent for the Germans on the Russian front and had twenty-eight murders to his credit; and now he wanted to work with us. He knew every person we wanted and could put his finger on them, just like that. That was our only real cloak-and-dagger operation. He joined us on the condition that he could be disguised. So we put him in a Canadian uniform, dyed his hair, and gave him dark glasses. We knew he was very dangerous. Of course, first we had to win his confidence, and among other things that meant somebody had to sleep in the same room with him. I volunteered to do it—no one else wanted to— and stuck my side arm under my pillow and went to sleep. I had a good sleep. He did his work for us but when the time came for us to leave, we had no choice but to lock him up. He was too dangerous.

In the fall of 1945 before we left the country, the area security officer and I went up to Amsterdam to turn over all our information to the former members of the Dutch underground who were now active as Dutch security agents. You should have seen these people—some of them looked like they were good pool hall material. They were mostly young, in their teens and early twenties, with long hair. But they sure knew their stuff—they were the best.

R.F. Sneyd

O Canada

Reverend Bob Sneyd became minister of the Calvary Baptist Church in Toronto in 1931. After the outbreak of war, he volunteered for the chaplaincy service and went overseas in 1940. He served as senior chaplain first with the 2nd Infantry Division and then with the 5th Armoured Division until his return to Canada in July 1945. The Reverend Sneyd occupied the pulpit of Calvary Baptist Church until his retirement in 1974.

At the end of the war I was serving with the 5th Armoured Division, which had the task of cleaning up the northeast corner of the Netherlands. The last place to fall was Delfzijl, the little port across from Emden, Germany. After the fighting ceased, we were stationed in Groningen. It was there that I met a German chaplain. There was an enemy hospital in the city with about a thousand patients in it, and I had been ordered to visit the chaplain and find out what he needed to perform his duties. It gave me a strange feeling to visit the hospital and walk among hundreds of men in enemy uniforms. The commanding officer of the hospital invited me up to his room for a cup of coffee and introduced me to the chaplain, a Lutheran minister from Berlin. I told them that they would be well cared for and informed the chaplain that I was there to provide him with what he needed for the discharge of his duties—burial sites for German soldiers, supplies for communion, and so on.

After a while we began to talk about the war in general, and I asked them what they thought about some of their leaders. I asked about Goering; they laughed, told a funny story about Goering, and said that he was a real clown. I asked about some other German figures, and it went on like this until I finally came to the crucial question: What did they think of Hitler? "Aaah," was all they could say, "der Fuehrer." After all they had been through and seen, they still had this reverence for Hitler, the chaplain being no exception.

In Groningen we were billetted in a little park surrounded by barbed wire in order to keep the civilians away and to prevent infiltration by any enemy troops that could still be found wandering around the city. There was a guard posted at the gate, and one day he came in with a Dutchman and told me that the man wanted to speak with me. I can't remember the gentleman's name but he identified himself as the organist and carillonneur of the famous church in Groningen, the Martini Kerk, and he requested my attendance at an entertainment to be held that evening at his apartment. Even though I was on duty, I made the time to go. The organist had invited some of his colleagues and musically I was absolutely swamped—way over my head.

One question he asked me was if I had any books on Canadian music. The Dutch were very anxious to learn anything they could about Canada. But I told him: "Well, you don't go into action carrying music books with you." So he asked me to tell him about any significant Canadian music that I knew. I mentioned several pieces, and hummed parts of them, but then he asked what was our national anthem. I said our anthem was the same as the British one, God Save the King, and he asked if we had no national song. So I said: "How would you like O Canada?" And he thought that was fine. I began humming it, and he took his pencil and a piece of paper and began splashing down the notes. By the time I had finished, he had put in his own harmony and began playing the anthem on the piano as if he had the printed music right in front of him—that was the kind of musician he was.

In Britain during the war there had been no church bells rung; anytime you heard the church bells, that was a sign of invasion. The same thing had been true in the Netherlands. The Germans allowed no bells to be rung during the war as they were considered a sign of general alarm. Consequently, that beautiful carillon in the Martini Kerk had not been played for years. Therefore, for the Dutch people, the liberation also meant the liberation of their worship and their music. On the last day of the war, we received the message that all offensive actions would cease at 0800 hours the next day, on the morning of May 5. At this time, there were thousands of Canadian soldiers stationed throughout the flat countryside all around Groningen, and

because of the terrain you could hear the church carillon at a distance. Well, on the day of the ceasefire, the carillon of the Martini Kerk could be heard again and the first piece to be played was O Canada. You should have seen the looks on the faces of the soldiers when they heard that music and realized it was their national song.

The Dutch were very sentimental about the Canadian soldiers. While we were in Groningen, I established a cemetery near the main road into the city, in a beautiful park. The chaplains brought their dead down to this little spot, to a burial place on the side of a hill above a small lake. At times the Dutch civilians made it almost impossible for us to bury our men. When we carried a soldier in on a stretcher for burial there would often be so many civilians milling around that you would have to push them aside to get to the grave. The Dutch had a lot of feeling for these Canadian boys and literally hundreds would show up for the burial services.

In the final days of the fighting, in our swing towards Delfzijl, two of our regiments had taken a number of casualties, maybe eight or ten fellows killed. The regiments' chaplains had buried the men in a corner of a field out in the country near a farmhouse, and one day I took a trip from Groningen to take a look at those graves. When I was there I saw two little girls come out of the farmhouse, go out in the field and pick daisies and other wild flowers which they then took over to the burial spot and placed in a tin can over each grave. And every day they put fresh flowers on each grave. In this act you could see the appreciation of even the smallest Dutch children for the soldiers who had laid down their lives for the liberation of the Netherlands.

On the evening of the official cease-fire, I went around Groningen and visited with at least half a dozen ministers I had met in the city, including a Baptist minister and a number of clergymen of the Dutch Reformed church. I returned to our headquarters at about ten o'clock at night, and there I found waiting for me a schoolmaster who had invited me to a victory night feast. I had forgotten about it completely, but I went in and changed my clothes, and then went out with him again. He led me through the city's downtown streets, around the canals and buildings, through a series of steep stairways and halls, into a room which had been used by the underground as a hiding place for people who had been trying to avoid capture by the Nazis. There were about sixty people in the room, all of whom had been involved in the concealment of fugitives, and when I arrived, they all stood up and sang God Save the King—I was obviously the honoured guest. These people had promised each other that on the day the war ended they would stay up all night and feast. There was no drink—just sixteen courses of food, half of which were made up of Canadian Army rations—with little entertainments between the courses. During the war, there had been strict curfews, and if the Dutch went out at night and did anything after the curfew hour had passed, they had to stay out the whole night. And that's what we did. I spent the whole evening there, returning to my quarters only at six o'clock in the morning.

When I returned to Canada, I brought back with me a lasting remembrance of my war experiences. This particular story actually began in September 1940 when I visited Westminster Abbey in London with a chaplain who was a friend of mine. The night before our visit, London had experienced its first night blitz, and some of the less important stained glass windows in the Abbey had been damaged. And while my friend and I stood there, in front of the tomb of the Unknown Warrior, as dramatic as it may seem, a piece of glass floated down from one of the damaged windows and landed right in front of us upon the black stone of the tomb. I picked it up and said to my friend: "The Lord is good to his own. I am going to start a collection of stained glass during this war." That was my first piece, and from then on, everywhere I went, I looked for broken glass. I didn't gather all of it myself; some of it was brought to me from damaged churches by men in my own unit, and some of it was gathered by other chaplains, but most of it I picked up myself. In Britain I must have picked up fragments from two hundred churches, and I continued this collection as we passed through France and Belgium, and went on into Holland and Germany.

Some of the fragments I gathered are extremely old. I was at Chichester Cathedral a half hour after it was bombed, arriving just as the verger was shovelling glass into a wheelbarrow for disposal; there I picked up a piece of glass showing the King offering frankincense from the Epiphany window. I also got a piece from Canterbury Cathedral. I collected glass from twenty-six different places in the Netherlands, including a fragment from a synagogue window in Nijmegen, and a beautiful head of Christ from the cathedral in 's Hertogenbosch.

I stored all these fragments in steel ammunition cases, brought them back to Canada, and put them away for a while. In the early fifties, when our new church was built, I asked the architect to leave a place in the tower for a memorial window. Two or three years later, after the completion of the building, a stained glass artist named Charles Taylor brought me a design for the window based on a suitable idea, and the window was built. The design, which incorporates many of the glass fragments I brought back from Europe, is based upon my experiences there and conveys a feeling of affirmation of life and of faith that grew out of my war service.

The Reverend Sneyd in front of the church window incorporating stained-glass fragments gathered during his years of service as an army chaplain.

Public Archives Canada, DND 51972 / M.M. Dean

When the surrender was announced, the Germans maintained their discipline and cooperated with the Canadian troops. Here German soldiers line up to surrender their weapons at a depot in the Amsterdam area.

(Opposite above) Bicycles seized from the Hermann Göring Division.

(Opposite below) The 5th Armoured Division on parade in Groningen.

German prisoners wash up by a stream in Harlingen while waiting to depart for home.

Public Archives Canada, DND 53199 / J.M. Smith

An army captain takes a bride in Groningen.

Chapter Four

The Wild Summer of 1945

As the month of May drew to an end the most urgent tasks that had faced the First Canadian Army lay behind it. The relief of the civilian population was no longer its responsibility, having passed to the Netherlands Military Authority. Operation "Eclipse," the concentration of German troops and materials, and the repatriation of the troops, was near completion. Increasingly the army faced problems of discipline and morale among the ranks, and the difficulties that arose from proximity to a large and woefully deprived population.

At the close of hostilities the morale of the troops was excellent. Senior officers feared, however, that boredom would set in as soldiers waited for repatriation. General Crerar pointed out to commanders on May 8 that a very difficult task awaiting them was "man-management." *Esprit de corps* must not be lost in the days ahead: "Commanders must devote a great deal of imaginative thought and energy to the utilization of ways and means which will revive and strengthen this essential possession." Organized sports and recreation, education, and continued training would all play important parts in the attempt to maintain a well disciplined force.

If boredom constituted one threat to discipline, fraternization with civilians was another. Fraternization, of course, had its positive side. Netherlanders were deeply grateful to the men who had come from a distant country and risked their lives in order to bring liberation. This particular enterprise had scarcely been in the soldiers' minds when they enlisted, but they could nevertheless take credit for it. They were welcomed into large numbers of Dutch homes. *Gezelligheid*, a Dutch word that encompasses companionableness and coziness, was extended to sometimes uncomprehending Canadians. But many eagerly accepted the invitations. Cut off from their own home life, they enjoyed sharing that of others. And they quickly learned to respond to dinner invitations by bringing canned meat, tea or coffee, chocolate and cigarettes. Their hosts often had little to offer in the way of food, and cigarettes were always appreciated.

So were the stories that the Canadians told. They came as wandering knights, bearing tales of exciting events and far-away places. The English and French languages were well enough understood that the knights could always find an audience, at least in the early weeks. Throughout the summer and autumn of 1945 the Entertainment Committee of the Netherlands, founded by civilians, helped to bring soldiers and Netherlanders together at functions of various kinds. Indeed no one needed much excuse for a celebration during the warm months, when the euphoria of liberation lingered. Neighbourhood feasts and dances were common.

Yet, welcome as the contacts with civilians were, other aspects of civilian-military relations tended to undermine military discipline. The Netherlands at the end of the war was dirt-poor. The country had been systematically exploited by the Germans, and what wealth remained had been redistributed towards farmers and black marketeers. There were exceptions to this rule, but especially in the cities many middle-class people

130

had lost their disposable assets during that dreadful final winter. In the lower social strata starvation meant that many people were too weak to put in a day's work, a state that persisted for weeks. Although official rations increased, they were still far from adequate in nutritional terms even by the middle of the summer. "Earning a living" was not easy. Under the strange circumstances of that time—"the wild, crazy summer of '45," one Dutch writer has called it—many took to more or less subtle forms of begging from the soldiers.

Initially many Canadians cheerfully shared their goods, especially cigarettes. Even as fighting was still taking place around Groningen, Dutch authors J.J. Leeninga and Jac. Westra noted, soldiers found time to give away chocolate and cigarettes. "Alas, this was destined to be the beginning of an importunate mendicancy that would take on ever more objectionable forms." But while some Netherlanders were embarrassed by it, at the outset many Canadians seem to have found the near-universal craving for tobacco products rather endearing. An indulgent attitude was soon joined by a more commercial outlook however. Civilians wanted cigarettes not just for themselves but for what they would fetch in the black market. "The black market flourishes to an alarming degree," the head of the SHAEF mission to the Netherlands wrote; and in it cigarettes were a sort of reserve currency.

Civilian confidence in the heavily inflated paper currency of the wartime administration was minimal. It was widely assumed that the returning government would reform the currency, probably sooner rather than later (it did so in September). In the meantime many people were reluctant to hold large quantities of paper money. They seized upon goods that could readily be turned into cash, and among them Canadian cigarettes, in packages or cartons, were very popular, not least because virtually no other cigarettes were available.

Because the black market was illegal, and dealers in it subject to prosecution, a wide spread existed between the buying and selling price of cigarettes. The former seems soon to have stabilized around one guilder a piece (the official exchange rate was one guilder = 40 cents Canadian), whereas the latter, paid by people who had no access to Canadians selling cigarettes, fluctuated around five guilders a piece. A skilled labourer

Parades were the order of the day. This one (opposite) by the 3rd Canadian Infantry Division in Utrecht marked the first anniversary of D-Day.

A mother and child watch the parade from curbside.

WHEN ♂ DROP A CIGARETTE IN HOLLAND!

might earn forty guilders a week, an unskilled labourer perhaps twenty-five, a domestic servant even less. The interest in dealing in cigarettes scarcely needs further explanation.

Canadians were under orders not to sell goods to civilians or barter with them, but the opportunities to do so were tempting. Some saw a chance to lay their hands on jewelry or antiques at very low cost. A soldier's relatives could send him 1000 cigarettes for three dollars; his return on them in the black market was the equivalent of $400. He could not exchange his illicit guilders for dollars, but he could buy valuables to be shipped home. A few did precisely that. Many more servicemen, not as entrepreneurially inclined or simply less greedy, exchanged cigarettes in order to be able to drink very cheaply in the military clubs and messes. Paymasters soon found to their annoyance that they were getting far more guilders back than had been issued to the troops.

There was little they or anyone else could do. Illegal though the trade was, the risks of being caught were small. A military commission of inquiry appointed by General Simonds found early in 1946 that "the great majority of the Canadians in Holland habitually sold cigarettes to the civilian population, and while this was generally known it was impracticable with the Provost forces available to curb the practice. . . ." Of course, many soldiers also used cigarettes to help, please or reward their Dutch acquaintances and friends.

One commodity that many soldiers tried to obtain with their cigarettes was hard liquor. Only the officers', warrant officers', and sergeants' messes were supplied with liquor; the other ranks had to make do with Belgian or British beer. (There was no Dutch beer available in May, and what was brewed over the summer was of low quality and in any case insufficient to supply civilian wants.) In the outside world liquor was rare and costly, for Dutch distilleries had nothing in stock. What was available was usually alcohol of very dubious quality: rotgut at best, lethal at worst. More than one soldier died that summer as a consequence of drinking methylated spirits.

Not surprisingly those who had access to liquor were sometimes tempted to put it to other than internal use. The officer who from June 1945 served as head of the Amenities Control Committee later told the commission of inquiry: "I was considered to be the biggest liquor dealer in [northwest Europe] . . . We never did acquire enough liquor to keep the thirst of the Canadian Army satisfied . . . I knew liquor was dynamite. The black market prices in Amsterdam were fantastically high and I trusted no one." However, he did occasionally sell bottles to fellow officers or to civilian members of the Entertainment Committee of the Netherlands, at prices which reflected the low cost per glass in the military clubs. Mess officers no doubt did the same. At least one commanding officer testified that officers quite commonly used liquor in order to obtain goods from civilians which they could not obtain in any other way.

Canadian dealings in the black market annoyed many Netherlanders. When currency reform was introduced by taking out of circulation all large-denomination notes, there was a definite public feeling that, along with black marketeers, soldiers who had accumulated quantities of paper money by shady means had got their just deserts. Rumours sprang up, however, that Canadians had been enabled to convert large amounts of currency into goods just before the reform. By mid-October General Guy Simonds, Crerar's successor as Commander-in-Chief of the Canadian Forces in the Netherlands, thought it advisable to order that the Dutch press be fully informed: no Canadians had been warned of the impending reform. He hoped that this would end the rumours.

Throughout 1945 cigarettes were central to the exchange relationship that grew up between soldiers and civilians. To say that they dominated the entire relationship would be an exaggeration. And the relations were close, even intimate. Most of the soldiers were located in the central, eastern and northern provinces, away from the most heavily populated areas. But nowhere was it easy to accommodate large groups of soldiers. Many lived in close proximity to civilians. There were efforts to keep too many of them from going to the most popular leave centre in the Netherlands, Amsterdam, but this added to the pressure on facilities in other recreation centres. Among the towns and cities that drew servicemen from the surrounding areas were Assen, Groningen, Harlingen and Leeuwarden in the north, Almelo, Arnhem, Deventer, Enschede, Nijmegen and Zwolle in the east, Amersfoort, Apeldoorn, Barneveld, Hilversum and Utrecht in the centre.

The Canadians lived among the Netherlanders longer than had been expected. With a shortage of transatlantic shipping repatriation was slower than had been hoped for. While they waited, the bulk of five divisions and numerous support services were concentrated in the Netherlands. The movement out was slow: out of a total of 170,000 men who entered the country, only 16,000 had left by the end of June, 59,000 by the end of August.

In spite of frequently successful efforts to keep the soldiers occupied and entertained, to educate them about the country they were staying in and to prepare them for demobilization, men got bored. Many were still in their late teens and early twenties;

Soldiers board a train at Nijmegen to begin the journey home. Under the point system for repatriation, those that had been overseas the longest were the first to be sent back to Canada.

As much as they liked the Netherlands, these soldiers were obviously happy to be repatriated. The words scribbled on the window of the door of the train are "Tokyo, Japan." This may indicate that these men had volunteered for duty in the Pacific. Soldiers who did so were given a month's leave in Canada, but by the time the leave was over, the war with Japan had been virtually concluded.

some had wives and families in England or Canada. In the Netherlands they were merely marking time.

Irritation also mounted among civilians as the months passed. Increasingly they resented the military occupation of factories, schools, houses, swimming pools, movie theatres and restaurants at a time when such facilities were in short supply. Some came to resent the soldiers because of their comparative wealth; others because they seemed to drink a lot or drove their vehicles at excessive speeds. Above all, many Netherlanders became critical of the relations between the Canadians and Dutch women.

In June General Crerar showed himself worried about Dutch reactions to a protracted Canadian presence. "If friendly relations are to be maintained during this trying period," he informed commanders, "then every officer and man must conduct himself correctly." Offences against civilians were to be heavily punished and to be redressed wherever possible. "All Commanders will ensure that all ranks are aware of the special responsibility now placed upon them in the interests of their country, of so behaving that, when they leave Holland, they leave behind true and grateful friends, prepared to work in close harmony with Canada in the years to come." Senior officers recognized the need for good public relations, and the PR service regularly issued releases to both the Dutch and Canadian press that emphasized the army's positive contributions to Dutch welfare.

The vital Canadian role in transporting food and fuel was understandably emphasized in the early phase. But on July 1 even this task passed to the Dutch authorities. Whether another role in assisting civilians might be found was a question that crossed the minds of both General Crerar and Major-General J.G.W. Clark, head of the SHAEF mission in the Netherlands. Crerar wrote to Clark on July 9: "It is likely that we will have many troops with little to do and if this surplus energy can be diverted to the task of simple rehabilitation . . . I feel it would be of benefit to all. Local assistance to agriculture is another idea which is being considered now."

The upshot of this was the use of Canadian soldiers in clearing war damage, especially to canals and bridges where special equipment was necessary which was not generally available to the local authorities. Care had to be taken not to do work that could be done by civilians, not to undermine the position of wage labourers in agriculture. Thus Canadians who worked on farms were not paid by the farmers. Instead the latter had to place the money they would otherwise have had to pay for labour into a charitable fund administered by the Dutch government.

The greatest success seems to have been an inter-city bus service for civilians laid on in late August. Initially the Dutch rejected such a service because neither they nor the Canadians wanted to shoulder liability in case of an accident. It was hard to ignore the need for such a service however. By mid-summer rail service was still rudimentary; there was no public transportation by road or highway. A military bus service existed, but it was not open to civilians. Eventually the problem of liability was resolved by having passengers sign a release form as they got on. During the first six days of service a reported 52,000 civilians made use of the new opportunity to travel between some of the major cities of the country. For the length of its existence, into the late autumn, the service continued to be popular.

The Dutch appreciated help of this kind. But no degree of helpfulness could

A soldier helps farmers harvest wheat. Special wage arrangements were made so that the assistance given by Canadian troops was not used to undermine the positions of Dutch agricultural labourers.

The soldiers continued to hold parties for Dutch children. These youngsters had been treated to an hour-long program of comic films before being fed sweets at a sergeants' mess in Utrecht.

neutralize growing unhappiness about the relations between soldiers and young women.

From the Canadian point of view the only problematic aspect of the relationship was medical. When in mid-May the 3rd Infantry Division was moved from Germany into the Netherlands, in an operation appropriately called "Fraternize," the divisional historian wrote: "As a result of our move into friendly country it is expected that unless definite steps are taken to point out the dangers of VD this disease will increase." It was evidently expected that boys would be boys.

But to what extent would girls be girls? Although a woman had reigned since 1890, the Netherlands before the war was a male-dominated country, conservative in its codes of social and sexual behaviour. Religion, particularly in its Reformed and Roman Catholic versions, still had a strong influence. In the southern Netherlands that influence was largely undiluted, as soldiers who spent the winter of 1944-45 there can testify. In the north, however, the war, and particularly its last long winter, had a significant effect on behaviour, perhaps particularly where younger women were concerned.

Women had become the providers, hunters for food at a time when many men were in Germany or dared not show themselves for fear of being sent into German war service. At the end of the war many Dutch men were still absent. Those who were around were thin, weak, badly dressed, poor and quite unattractive. By contrast, Canadian soldiers were weather-bronzed, muscled heroes of liberation who were presumably ready to show a girl a good time and had the wherewithal to provide it. And many women must have felt they were entitled to one. Those who had resisted German servicemen for years may have been peculiarly vulnerable. (On the other hand, one of the minor scandals of the period was that some young women who had consorted with German soldiers took little time, usually no more than it took their shaven heads to regain some hair, to find Canadian friends.) "We were no competition for the Canadians," one Dutch man, then nineteen years old, has said. "Let's face it, after what we had been through the Canadians looked delicious," one war bride remembered. Gratitude and sexual attraction combined to drive Dutch women into Canadian arms. A Dutch journalist has commented: "Dutch men were beaten militarily in 1940, sexually in 1945."

A postcard shows the affection of the Dutch for the Canadian soldiers.

THE GERMANS STOLE OUR FOOD,
THE CANADIANS OUR HEART!

Canadian soldiers and Dutch women got along famously. No doubt there were many of the latter who kept their distance, but there were more than enough who sought out the conquering heroes, all 170,000 of them. "There were many attractive young ladies around who showed great interest in us Canadians," Ben Dunkelman has written, "and our parties—making up for lost time—were truly memorable events." One sore point with many civilians was that Dutch men were excluded from them. Lurid stories did the rounds about the Canadian parties, and although there was probably a lot of exaggeration in the tales, the celebrations do seem to have been appropriately Dionysian. From all accounts the Canadians liked to drink and loved to dance.

Before the war Dutch society had been distinctly prudish. Many Netherlanders, witnessing what they considered to be "loose" behaviour, such as necking in public places, thought that something new and deplorable was taking place. They were inclined to take for granted that soldiers would be sexually active, but they were very critical of Dutch women who gave the appearance of being so. From the beginning there were plenty of Netherlanders inclined to think ill of those who dated Canadians.

One belief was that some women were selling themselves for cigarettes. "When a girl received a package of cigarettes from her Canadian friend, she could sell them for a guilder apiece. . . ," Dutch authors Leeninga and Westra noted disdainfully. "Under the circumstances many of these girls did not even consider taking a job. They could earn the money much more easily." A cartoon drawn in 1945 by a Hilversum artist, Jan Nieuwenhuis, depicted a handsome soldier leering at a pretty woman and asking: "How many cigarettes?"

From all sides came warnings to women not to throw themselves away. "Trees heeft een Canadees," was the title of a popular song that summer: "Trish has a Canadian." Its tone was critical, and it ended by asking how she would fare once her "boy" should have departed for his home in Ottawa. Much sterner was a piece of doggerel poetry, "Meisje let op je zaak" (Girl, look after yourself), which did the rounds in the late summer. It explicitly took the girls to task for seducing soldiers for the sake of a package of cigarettes, a chocolate bar, a drink or a can of corned beef. What would be left of their good name?

      . . .

Many who collaborated with the Germans
Bear the stigma now;
Girl, you also are a traitor
Against the honour of the Netherlands!
People come and go;
Tommy will do so too.
Don't think that he'll take you with him;
Girl, have you thought of that?

Then no Dutch boy
Will even look at you
Because, so to say,
You left him out in the cold.
Be good to our liberators;
Theirs is a great accomplishment,
But think, there are limits:
Girl, look after yourself!

The more immediate consequences which many Netherlanders feared were unwanted pregnancies and venereal diseases. As to the former, a joke did the rounds: "In twenty years, when another world war may have broken out, it will not be necessary to send a Canadian expeditionary force to the Netherlands. A few ships loaded with uniforms will be enough." This was an exaggeration. There *was* an increase in illegitimacy however. More than 7,000 illegitimate births were recorded in 1946, compared with approximately a third that number in the last "normal" year, 1939. It is interesting that legitimate births in 1946 totalled 277,000, easily the highest annual figure in Dutch history, and almost a hundred thousand more than in 1940. It has been suggested that a proportion of this baby boom was half-Canadian, but that is impossible to substantiate. A few moralists did complain in 1945 that some married men encouraged their wives to date Canadians, presumably with the object of obtaining cigarettes, canned goods and so on.

There were occasional reports of startling rises in the rates of venereal disease among

A cartoon from a book by a Dutch artist, Jan Nieuwenhuis, depicts what the Dutch regarded as the seamier side of the cigarette economy fuelled by the Canadian presence in the post-war Netherlands.

women. An article in *De Ochtendpost* on August 4, 1945 claimed that in Amsterdam alone two thousand women were suffering from syphilis. Because penicillin was not yet available to the civilian health authorities, such reports were worrisome. But the tendency among civilians to blame the spread of the disease on the soldiers were mistaken. The army was almost fanatic on the subject of prophylaxis. There had in fact been a steep increase in the incidence of VD in the Netherlands during the war. For example, a public health official in Groningen told a joint civilian-military committee in August that, where in 1938 there had been two known cases of syphilis in the area and four in 1939, by 1944 there were 334. He linked this to the deterioration in public health services as well as the growing demoralization of the people during the German occupation.

At this meeting a medical officer with the 5th Armoured Division confirmed that the incidence of VD among the troops had risen greatly in the Netherlands: "Perhaps it is because the Dutch and Canadians get along very well together." In August in the Groningen area 252 infected soldiers had named 252 different women as contacts, indicating at least a certain degree of monogamy.

At the meeting other subjects for discussion included the protection of minors—there were disturbing reports of teenaged girls dancing nude at military parties—and illegitimacy. The Canadians warned the civilians that the Canadian government assumed no responsibility for illegitimate children and would not constrain the fathers to do so. Interestingly there were no references to rape as a problem.

Dutch official efforts to try to control the situation seem to have been minimal. This is not surprising, for the possibility of conflict with the Canadian military authorities was very real. Rather more was done privately, especially by religious leaders and organizations. Thus the Christian Association of Friends of the Soldiers and the YMCA sought to bring young people together in "wholesome" surroundings and under proper supervision. Others too hoped by gentle persuasion to discourage women from "degrading" themselves and their Canadian friends through too liberal an intercourse.

Some went further. Sporadic attempts were made to keep women from dating Canadians. Occasionally there were threats of reprisals once the soldiers should have departed, as in the small town of Culemborg, south of Utrecht, in June. Similar occurrences in July in Utrecht itself and in Almelo troubled senior officers. They did not want the Canadian newspapers to get hold of such stories, which might reflect unfavourably on the army back home.

In August the weekly *Vrij Nederland* carried an article asserting that the "sexual hunger" of the Canadians was a direct menace to both public health and morality, and implored parents to try to preserve a distance between their daughters and military men. Religious figures increasingly decried the dancing which seemed to lead to greater intimacy and urged young women not to attend dances. Many people thought this went too far; it seemed inhospitable and ungrateful. Efforts to stop the dating were generally deprecated. But could not young women simply behave respectably?

Probably a good deal of the behaviour ascribed to women was the result of projection. At the same time, standards of behaviour were shifting, particularly in the urban centres of the largely Protestant north. The war had affected traditional notions of right and wrong, had undermined parental authority, had thrust younger women into positions of unusual importance. To limit their freedom in the aftermath of war, in the euphoria of that liberation summer, was not really feasible. Among the farming population and in the smaller towns and villages, possibly; in the cities, no.

The circumstances were unusual; people behaved in ways to which Netherlanders have since become accustomed, but which at the time disturbed many of them. Many soldiers too behaved in unaccustomed ways. Mostly young men, with little or no sexual experience when they left Canada and only limited opportunity since then to change that state of affairs, they went a little wild that summer. Yet it would be foolish to assume, as some worried Netherlanders did, that Canadian soldiers were satyrs and that more than casual contact between them and Dutch women necessarily led to intimate sexual relations. The personal moral codes of many men and women surely precluded this. Moreover, a number of lasting relationships developed. Love pointed in the direction of marriage.

Yet when we have allowed for the tendency of many Dutch people in 1945 to suspect what they considered to be "the worst," it remains true that, along with Canadian involvement in the black market, the relations between soldiers and women constituted a major source of irritation. It affected civilian attitudes to soldiers and helped to bring about at least a couple of major brawls between the two groups. One took place in Zwolle in mid-August, another in Utrecht in September.

Over-consumption of alcohol contributed to both fights. There was a deterioration in the deportment of the troops, General Simonds noted at a staff conference on October 15. There was too much drinking and consequent disorderliness, too much illegal use of army vehicles, too much speeding and too many accidents. Standards of dress and saluting were becoming lax. John Morgan Gray later remembered:

> It was time to go. We had grown slack and we were wearing out our welcome. The smart, well-disciplined troops that had waved and smiled their way into Dutch hearts and homes in the delirious days following VE Day had become just another Occupation Army, not hated yet, but standing in the way of a return to normal life in Holland. The race-tracks, the theatres, the playing fields, the dance halls were for Canadian troops, where Dutch girls might be entertained but not Dutch men. A Nijmegen paper finally said in a resounding editorial what many had been muttering: the gist of it was, "Let them go home. We are grateful to them, but let them go home. We won't forget these nice smiling boys, and they will always have our good wishes and our gratitude, but let them go home. They are not happy here and we are no longer happy to have them; so let them go home."

Canadian soldiers shared that wish. Repatriation went too slowly. By the end of November almost 70,000 men still remained in the Netherlands, but most of these left in December and January. The Headquarters, Canadian Forces in the Netherlands, was disbanded on May 31, 1946; the Canadian presence had ceased to be noticeable to most civilians several months earlier.

In the end not a few Netherlanders were almost as happy to see the Canadians leave as they had been to see them arrive. Nevertheless on both sides earnest and often successful efforts had been made to maintain good relations. Civilians entertained the soldiers in many ways; the military, too, frequently acted as hosts to civilians. There were many small functions and some large ones, such as the festival that the 2nd Division held for 20,000 people at Soesterberg airfield, near Utrecht, in early September. It included a circus, a rodeo, horse show, midway, sports events and, in the evening, a dance. Worth noting also are the many St. Nicholas parties that the military units arranged for Dutch children in December of 1944 and 1945. Entertainments of this kind are part of the reason why today both Canadians and Netherlanders remember that time with pleasure.

Repatriation re-united some soldiers with their wives; it separated others from them, at least for a time. The Canadian government subsequently paid the passage to Canada of 1,886 Dutch war brides and 428 children. (This compares with almost 45,000 British war brides, 649 Belgian and 100 French; the Dutch contingent was thus the second largest.) In addition, an unknown number of Dutch women married Canadians after 1946 as a result of their meeting each other during the liberation period.

Not all of the war brides actually come to Canada. A few of the marriages had come apart before transportation could be arranged. No doubt such instances confirmed the military authorities in the view that they had been wise to make marriage difficult. "The general policy is to dissuade members of the Canadian Army from marriage in foreign lands," an official directive drafted late in 1944 stated. "Marriage with a person of a different country, particularly by young soldiers, and where there is a difference of religion, is open to obvious risks of unhappiness. . . ." Commanders were instructed to refuse consent outright if they were not "satisfied that a reasonable basis for a happy marriage exists and in any event a four months' waiting period will be imposed between the date of the granting of permission to marry and the date on which the marriage may be solemnized, unless there are circumstances [such as pregnancy] making this delay undesirable or unnecessary." In the Netherlands the woman had to tender a certificate of good moral behaviour, usually obtained from a minister or priest. In addition, commanding officers had to get a certificate of the woman's political reliability from the Political Search Service of the Dutch government or the Bureau of National Safety.

Did the impulse to marry come primarily from the women? We cannot say positively that it did. One Army chaplain, however, serving with the 5th Armoured Division, stated during the aforementioned civilian-military meeting in Groningen that "there seems to be an undue haste on the part of Dutch girls to marry Canadians, and . . . this was also evident on the part of the parents, regardless of the fact that the soldier's background etc. was entirely unknown to them." A new life in a new country, married to a man who already had roots there—the notion had considerable appeal. Quite possibly some of the soldiers had inflated their social status a bit in order to make themselves more appealing. In the book *Herbie!*, a cartoon by Bing Coughlin shows Herbie, a sort of Private Everyman, burying his head in his hands while a Dutch boy says to his gorgeous older sister: "Now that the war is over we'll be soon leaving for Uncle Herbie's big ranch in Toronto."

Whether Dutch war brides went to Canada for love or for a new country, or for a combination of the two, is ultimately a subject for idle speculation. Whatever the case, they constituted the first of many personal ties across the ocean established after the war. Many other emigrants were to follow. The country they left behind soon forgot the irritations associated with the Canadian presence. Large armies stationed among

PUBLIC ARCHIVES CANADA, DND 58247 / KEN BELL

civilians bring unavoidable problems with them; the deprived and demoralized condition of the Netherlands—no occupied country in northwestern Europe suffered more during the war—compounded the problems. But the petty resentments soon vanished after the Canadians left.

In retrospect the wild summer of 1945, with all its excesses, came to be seen in a rosy light, as a time simply of new-found freedom and celebration. In T.S. Eliot's words, "age and forgetfulness sweeten memory." Relations between soldiers and civilians had on the whole been good. In time they came to seem even better than probably in fact they were.

A large number of the romantic relationships between Canadian soldiers and Dutch women, formed in the heady days following the liberation, ended in marriage.

Ann Simpson

Sister of Mercy

Ann Simpson (née Jaarsma) was working as a nurse in a hospital at Apeldoorn when it was liberated on April 17, 1945.

When I got back to the hospital, because I could speak English, I was assigned to the ward where wounded Canadian soldiers were being treated. Two days after the liberation, seven men were brought in with shrapnel wounds; one of them also had pneumonia and was burning up with fever. I was on night duty and had to make rounds to give out medication. I came to this man's bed and he asked me what I was giving him. I told him that one pill was an antibiotic and the other would make him sleep. Well, he looked at me and said he didn't want to sleep at all. He said to me that I was the prettiest nurse in the hospital and that he would much rather sleep during the day when I wasn't around and look at me all night. Of course, I went by the book, was very efficient, and told him that he was very flattering but that I would have to file a report, and it would look pretty silly if I put down "soldier prefers to look at nurse." He said, "You're right, but you're still the prettiest nurse in this hospital," and then he asked me to go out with him on a date when he would be released. I didn't like him that much, but in order to get him to take his medication I said okay. He was there three weeks but as far as I was concerned, he was just another patient. Then he was transferred to a British convalescent hospital; I said goodbye and before he left he reminded me of my promise, but I never thought that I would see him again.

A short time later, I asked for a leave of absence from the hospital. I was just exhausted, physically and mentally, and took on a private nursing job. I moved out of the hospital into the home of the patient I was caring for. About a month later, one night that I'll never forget, the bell rang at this home, the maid answered and said it was for me. Here was the hospital patient. I had trouble recognizing him because he was out of uniform. He reminded me of my promise to

Ann Simpson.

go out with him and said he had gotten my address from the hospital. At this point, I took another look at him and thought that he was good looking.

The first date was really something. We went to a Canadian army show and I couldn't understand a word of it; I just laughed when everybody else did. The one thing that impressed me on our first date was how courteous he was. He was really so polite and so thoughtful. That appealed to me and I guess that that's part of the reason I fell in love with him. He kept telling me that I was special. I think that had a lot to do with his experience in the hospital. When he was there, he was homesick and felt especially bad at night. I was always there to listen to him talk about his home and his family even if I didn't always understand what he was saying. I guess that's why I appealed to him.

In 1945, Ann Jaarsma married James Simpson, a private in the Royal Canadian Army Service Corps, and settled in Canada.

Wilhelmina Smith

A Ride in a Jeep

Wilhelmina (Willy) Smith (née de Jong) was 19 years old when the war began and worked as a secretary at a large factory in Amsterdam.

For weeks after the war we were all in a holiday mood—we still couldn't believe our good luck. About a month after the liberation, on a lovely day in June, I went out with one of my older sisters to meet another. We were walking on the street when along came a jeep with three Canadian officers in it. They passed us by slowly and the men said hello; since we were trying to improve our English, we said hello too. They turned around and parked, and my sister, who was always the matchmaker type, urged me to go over and see what they wanted. I wasn't all that eager, but she said: "Come on now. You can speak English." They said they had lost their way and told us they were stationed in Arnhem and were on leave in Amsterdam for the first time; then one of them asked me to be their guide and show them around the city. My sister told me to do it, and I thought they looked pretty nice and that it would be a real experience riding in a jeep. So I got into the front seat and showed them the city: the royal palace, the central station, and the art gallery with Rembrandt's paintings. And all the girls were looking at me, saying, "Isn't she lucky, sitting in a jeep?" So I felt pretty good.

I had to be home by four o'clock and when we got there, the officer who was driving asked if he could see me the following Wednesday night and take me to a dance. I said alright—I liked him and was kind of thrilled. He held my hand and was very charming. All three of the men wanted to date me and I felt kind of special, but I guess it was their first time on leave in Amsterdam and they hadn't met many Dutch girls yet. One of the men asked me to bring a date for him, and when I asked my girlfriend she thought it was a great idea; she was dying to try out her English on the soldiers.

Sure enough he showed up in the jeep the next Wednesday. When my date came upstairs to meet my sister, we sat down and

Wilhelmina Smith today (above) and at her wedding in 1945 in Amsterdam.

145

offered him a glass of vermouth. But then I thought of something—I was very practical—and said to him: "Something has occurred to me. I would like to know if you are a bachelor or married or engaged in Canada." He said he wasn't married, that he had some girlfriends at home, but that he was free. So I asked him to prove it. He showed me his army pay book which indicated he was a bachelor; well, that was okay and I could go out with him. And from then on he came from Arnhem all the way to Amsterdam three times a week to see me.

Wilhelmina de Jong married Captain Stuart Adam Smith in 1945, in the "Nieuwe Kerk" on the Dam Square in Amsterdam. They were the first Canadian couple to marry there, and then they settled in Toronto.

Herbert Gater

Obstacles to Marriage

Herbert Gater served in the Perth Regiment and met his wife, Willemina Brand, in the northern city of Groningen.

After the war ended, one of my jobs was the procurement of fresh food stuffs for my regiment. I went around to the farms driving a truck loaded with chocolate bars, cigarettes, bully beef, and I would trade them for fresh eggs, potatoes, carrots and beans. One day, I went to a farm where they couldn't understand me very well and they told me to come back that evening when there would be a girl there who spoke English. I thought that was just what I needed, so I went back that evening and met the girl who would later become my wife. From then on, I didn't have to go to any other farm.

Some months later when we decided to get married, the officers of my regiment tried to discourage me from going ahead. I guess part of the reason was that so many men wanted to marry European women. I had to go through

quite a routine. The padre took me aside and asked what I had promised this girl; he was afraid that I had told her I owned a ranch in Toronto and had all kinds of money. He warned me that I didn't know the girl well enough and that there was a language barrier. Well, I told him that my wife spoke perfect English. Then he asked me if I had made her pregnant; I said no, but she still had to go for an examination to prove that that wasn't the case. Finally I told them that she came from a very fine family and that we had made up our minds to get married. Then I had to go to see the justice of the peace in Leeuwarden and he also put me through a lot of questioning as to why I wanted to marry this girl. But they couldn't change my mind.

We had a beautiful wedding. There was an army guard of honour. The ceremony was at the town hall, with all the guests around a horseshoe-shaped table, the Canadian soldiers on one side and my wife's family on the other. The service was in English and Dutch. After the ceremony was over, all the soldiers threw Dutch guilders onto the floor and that was our present. I paid for the wedding with tobacco—eleven hundred cigarettes for the rings and the photographer, and cigarettes and chocolate to settle the hotel bill. After the wedding, we had only one day together and then I had to leave to return to Canada. My wife followed eleven months later. When I got home, my family was quite upset about the marriage; they could not understand why I had married a foreign girl. But after my wife arrived in Canada, things turned out fine.

Herbert and Willemina Gater with a souvenir flag taken after the German defeat at Delfzijl in the northern Netherlands.

Donald & Anne Davenport

Something Old, Something New

Donald Davenport enlisted in the Canadian army in January 1942, at the age of 19, and landed in Sicily two days after the invasion in 1943. After serving in Italy he was sent to Belgium in the fall of 1944 and finished the war with the 6th Royal Canadian Hussars in the Netherlands. In the city of Groningen he met the daughter of a postman, a dressmaker, Annie Lohr.

MR. DAVENPORT: I was out one night in Groningen with another soldier, when we met two girls on the street. We said hello and asked them where they were going. They didn't understand what we were saying so we decided to follow them. They went back to one of the girl's homes and we walked right in, went into the kitchen, shook hands with the parents and sister and brothers, said we were Canadians and introduced ourselves. We were soldiers and they didn't really worry. Then we went back to the camp and got chocolate bars and cigarettes and tea and coffee.

MRS. DAVENPORT: I couldn't understand why they were leaving so soon, but later they came back with a great big bag of food and we had a party. This was our liberation celebration. They stayed quite late and we were really happy.

Before they left my mother told them they could bring their laundry over. We really needed the soap and they were happy to get their washing done. When they came back for their clothes, one of them, Donald, asked me to go to a dance. I thought he was a nice-looking Canadian and was quite thrilled. I couldn't speak English and we communicated with our hands except for saying yes and no.

We went to this dance on a Saturday night, and there were a lot of Dutch girls standing outside the building waiting to get in. Soldiers could only enter with a date, and the girls hoped to get picked up at the door. We had a

good time dancing and tried to talk as much as was possible. After that Donald came back to see me quite often. I refused to walk through the park with him; some girls went there with Canadian soldiers and were looked down upon, and I didn't want anyone to say I was that kind of girl.

It wasn't too long before he asked me if I wanted to go to Canada with him and get married. I nearly fell over and said yes right away. My father liked him, maybe because of the cigarettes Donald brought when he visited. He brought cigarettes for my father and chocolate bars for my mother.

Donald and Anne Davenport at their wedding (above) and today (below).

147

When we decided to get married we had many arrangements to make. We had to see the mayor, and the army sent an officer to meet with me and my parents so that I could ask questions about the man I was going to marry. I asked about his background in Canada, his work and his family, if he had ever been in trouble with the police, if he was in good health. He had a good record. Then they told me that I had to go to a doctor and show my own health record; they also checked to make sure that I had not been a collaborator during the war. I also made sure that Donald was not married already, or separated or divorced.

MR. DAVENPORT: I had to ask our major for permission to get married and he said he would never say no. He said if we had made up our minds that he wished us the best of luck.

For the wedding we rented a cafe with a fair amount of cigarettes. The camp took up a collection for us and gave me a bag of food for our honeymoon. We bought sandwiches of cheese and ham for the wedding and got one bottle of cherry brandy. My mother sent material from Canada for my wife's wedding dress. My wife rented her veil and shoes. We arranged for four horse-drawn carriages to carry the wedding party; this custom was popular because cars had not been easily available during the war. We also put a wedding announcement in the paper, and because my wife was one of the first girls in Groningen to marry a Canadian soldier, there was a crowd of about five or six hundred people in the church.

MRS. DAVENPORT: My husband left for England in December 1945 and I was left behind. I made friends with other war brides and joined the Dutch wives' club. We got as much information as we could about when we would be leaving. That kept us happy. We were all in the same boat. Eventually we were told that we would be leaving in the spring or summer and that we would have to be ready to leave at twenty-four hours' notice. I kept my suitcase packed, and in July I got a telegram telling me to be ready to be picked up.

My mother had told all the neighbours that I was leaving the next morning and everybody turned out on the street to say goodbye. I felt a bit sad to leave my friends. A private car with a Canadian soldier as chauffeur, and with other war brides in the back seat, came to get me. I got in and waved goodbye. My mother was crying, my father was crying, and the neighbours were sad, and I waved and waved until I could not see them anymore.

From Groningen we were taken to The Hague where they put us up in a nice hotel with about three hundred other war brides from all over the country. Then we went to Rotterdam where we took a boat to England. We stayed one night in London and all our papers were checked again. Then we went to Liverpool to board the *Queen Mary* with the English war brides.

MR. DAVENPORT: I came home in January 1946 and found it strange. Canadian girls' accents all sounded strange—it made you feel kind of funny. After a while, I wished I had stayed in Europe with the occupation forces. At least, I would have been close to my wife. During the six months I was home alone, I went through money like it was going out of style.

MRS. DAVENPORT: I came to Toronto with only ninety dollars. The first thing I did was to go into a shoe store and buy myself a new pair of shoes. It was the first pair of shoes I had bought in more than four years, and I really liked having something new.

There was a housing shortage in Canada and we lived in a couple of rooms—it wasn't very much. I felt kind of sad. I was homesick for the first five years, but I tried not to let on. Each day when my husband went to work, I was left alone in our rooms; I couldn't speak English well and I was lonely. But soon they started a war brides' club, and then I got pregnant and that kept me busy. My husband bought me a sewing machine, and I began to knit and sew, and things became more normal. Then I began to like Canada better.

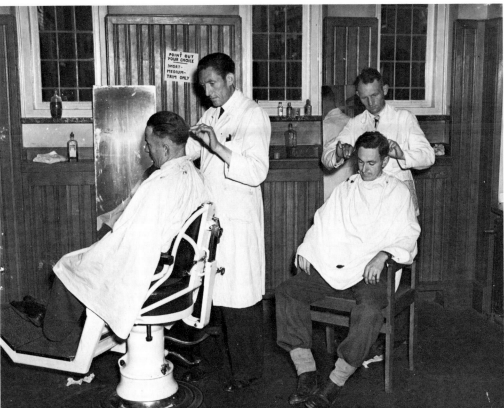

Soldiers congregated at the servicemen's clubs in each city, where they could get a free haircut or enjoy a drink.

Sports meets, like this one at Groningen in June 1945 (opposite above), were part of a large variety of activities designed to keep up the morale of soldiers who had to wait months for repatriation.

(Opposite below) The Perth Regiment holds a track and field day at Sneek.

(Left) Princess Juliana presents a prize to the South Saskatchewan Regiment's tug-of-war team.

(Below) At a sports meet, Dutch girls in native dress drink tea with the soldiers.

151

152

PUBLIC ARCHIVES CANADA, DND 57745 / KEN BELL

PUBLIC ARCHIVES CANADA, DND 58974 / KEN BELL

(Opposite above) A soldier in the Highland Light Infantry plays for a Dutch maiden at a regimental barbecue, and a "hillbilly" band performs in a show called the "Rainbow Review" prepared by the 5th Anti-Tank Regiment.

(Opposite below) One of the floats in a St. Jean Baptiste Day parade sponsored by Le Régiment de la Chaudière.

(Above) At its farewell party, the Highland Light Infantry staged a skit based on the famous comic strip "Li'l Abner."

(Left) The first St. Nicholas parade in Amsterdam since the outbreak of the war was held on December 1, 1945, with Canadian army jeeps carrying Dutch children in the procession.

PUBLIC ARCHIVES CANADA, DND 58721 / KEN BELL

Canadian soldiers and their fiancées at the first meeting of the Dutch Wives Club in Amersfoort.

Lester Sugarman

The Grandest Affair

Lester Sugarman was at university when the war began and tried unsuccessfully to enlist in the Medical Corps. He later joined an engineering unit as a private, went into Europe ten days after D-Day, and finished his service in the Netherlands as a staff sergeant.

After the war ended, I got separated from my unit when I was sent on a course; the rest of my unit went home. Upon my return to the Netherlands, I was sent to Grave. There wasn't much to do, and one of my jobs was that of education officer. I ran a rehabilitation project which involved sending people all over Europe for short courses at universities in Belgium and France, England and Denmark. The courses were two weeks long and I remember particularly an excellent one on the social history of Denmark. I ran this project from June to September.

I also did some work on getting vehicles and equipment sent back to Canada. The problem was that soldiers would sell the equipment that we were shipping inside vehicles. The Belgians didn't have any machinery, and when the vehicles went through Antwerp, everything would be ripped off. It was impossible to ship stuff back home on a secure basis. That was really an awful business.

The temptations for soldiers were fantastic. You could sell anything that was loose. The Belgians in particular wanted what we had. Equipment such as valve-grinding machinery for a garage was worth a fortune. It was easy to do: soldiers would be driving along, take a quick detour, or stop for a cup of coffee, and that was it. This wasn't for the sort of money you could make selling cigarettes—this was for big money. Some of the guys got caught. It was a moral dilemma for a lot of soldiers. We didn't know what was going to happen to the equipment and anyway a lot of it was surplus. I remember when I got home some very highly placed people who had sent back fancy cars were thrown into jail and disgraced. That sort of thing was going on at all levels.

After the war was over, we had so much time on our hands that it was easy to go AWOL for weeks. And when I met my wife there was no point in staying around camp doing menial jobs, like checking how much gasoline went into a truck, when I could go off and have a friend cover for me. Unfortunately one time I got caught; I really had picked the wrong time to leave. My number came up for me to go home and I wasn't at parade when my name was called. Luckily, the commanding officer just confined me to barracks, and that was that.

Things were different for the soldiers in the Netherlands simply because we were made so welcome. Most of the guys came from half-decent homes and knew what it was to treat a woman properly; and if they were treated properly in turn and invited into the homes of people, it was pretty hard to be a rotter. I don't think many guys forced women to do things they didn't want to do—it didn't have to be like that. Dutch men were so debilitated and their morale so low that they couldn't get angry. Except for the farmers and men in the underground, most Dutch men had had nothing to do all those years and became emasculated. They were either in hiding or in forced labour camps in Germany, and when they came back they felt horrible.

We were in Holland a long time and I think everybody found a place where he could feel at home. It was almost more comfortable than being in England. I know that a lot of Canadian boys resented many of the things they had seen in England—the way women were treated, the class distinctions—but not in the Netherlands. There were some stand-offish people in certain strata of society, but it had nothing to do with resentment of soldiers or Canadians.

I also don't think we ever met a more willing female population than we did in Holland. They were very warm; even the Dutch girls I had met in England were like that. They were just ready to give of themselves. They seemed so much earthier than most girls we had met previously, and they didn't get uptight about a lot of things. I think it was just the way Dutch women were, and reflected the way in which they had been brought up. And if they weren't constrained by religious or other taboos, sexual relations presented no problem.

I met my wife through a soldier who was my roommate. He had a sister who had married a Dutchman before the war, and after several weekend trips of searching Amsterdam, he found them. He wanted me to meet them, but I kept putting him off. In September the armed forces arranged a Jewish High Holiday service in Amsterdam. I was given leave and my roommate convinced me to go there for the service and to stay at his sister's house.

We went up to Amsterdam, bringing two full bags of food with us. My friend's sister lived in a huge house with no furniture left in it except one table, a couple of chairs, and mattresses on the floor. I was introduced to Tillie, the sister of my friend's brother-in-law. When I told them that I was going to a service, they ran around and got me a prayer shawl and prayer book and something to cover my head; I was very moved by this gesture. I asked them how to get to the service, and Tillie said she was going that way because she planned to attend a concert. My heart just melted and I asked if I could go with her—I hadn't been to a concert in over a year. So that's what I did; I went to the concert instead. Her mother was really wonderful to me, inviting me to eat and sleep at their house. I went back to Amsterdam practically every weekend, and Tillie and I got really involved.

It was a magic time. Amsterdam is a very romantic city—all the trees along the canals, the museums, the little stores and the walks we used to take—it was really heaven. I certainly wasn't considering marriage at the time—it was just the grandest affair that I'd ever had. Tillie was in a friendship circle of artists and professional people who had been through the war together, so there was lots of interesting conversation every weekend.

When they told me I had to go home, I knew that I didn't want to give this up. I knew I didn't want to stay in Holland, but I didn't want to leave either. It was ridiculous—I didn't know what I was going home to or what I was going to do with my life. Then I went to a wedding of a friend—I thought if he had the guts to do that, maybe I could think about it too. Then I tried the tactic of talking Canada down: I told Tillie how horrible Toronto was and how little there was to do in Vancouver. I was worried that she would never make it back home. But I didn't want to leave her, so we finally did it—we got married.

George Low

Absent with Leave

George Low enlisted in Toronto in 1943, was sent overseas the following year, and joined up with the 48th Highlanders of Canada in Utrecht in May 1945. Shortly after liberation, most of the regiment returned to Canada, and George Low was transferred to the Argyll and Sutherland Highlands. He returned to Canada in the fall of 1945.

At the end of May 1945, after a couple of weeks of duty guarding German prisoners, we were sent to Scheveningen, the magnificent resort town on the North Sea near The Hague. We had nothing to do and tried to fill in the days as best as we could. Mostly the padre would round us up and try to take us on trips. I could see that those who had been in the thick of the fighting were fed up and wanted to go home. But for me it was kind of interesting, because I could walk into The Hague and go sightseeing. Many of the guys had money taken from German prisoners—you weren't supposed to do that—but there was nothing to buy anyway. People were still desperate and would always ask you for things.

In the weeks after the war there were still severe food shortages, so we went on half-rations to help feed the populace. We were always a little hungry and pulling in our belts a bit. On many days when you went to the mess hall to eat something, kids would gather around; they wouldn't beg, they would just look at you pathetically. So you'd eat for a while, but then, when you had five and six-year-olds staring at every mouthful, you would finally take your sandwich, hand it to them, mutter to yourself and walk away. Many of us did that. We were on half-rations for a month or so until the food situation improved.

It was a boring time, so they were always moving us around—they didn't know what to do with us. We did a lot of marching every day to prepare for the victory parade in Rotterdam. After Scheveningen, we got transferred to Hilversum. We were still bored and took trips whenever we could. They used to

George Low.

tell us to show up for parade at nine o'clock in the morning unless it looked like it was going to rain. Well, in the morning the fellows would get up, and if they saw a few clouds in the sky, we wouldn't go on parade. But most of those days turned out to be beautiful. On days when the commanding officer showed up, the major in front of our platoons would say, "all present and accounted for" when he knew darn well that most of the men weren't there. He didn't care either.

One day when there were only a few of us out on parade, the commanding officer asked if anyone wanted to take a trip. He offered us the use of a storm craft, which was a flat-bottomed boat that could cross canals and rivers at high speed. He told us that we could go anywhere we liked in Holland as long as we returned in two weeks' time. I said to the fellow beside me that we should go—we hadn't done anything in days except sleep. Some of the fellows were wary about volunteering for anything because you never knew how it would turn out; but we stepped forward with a couple of other guys and, sure enough, they gave us a great big craft with a seventy-five horsepower motor and several cans of petrol. And away we went.

We had a marvelous time. We could exchange the empty petrol cans for full ones at any unit, and as far as food was concerned, we had nothing to worry about because we could step into the mess line of any regiment as long as we had our own mess tins with us. The trip took us north to Groningen, over to Leeuwarden and then back down again. We came back in just over two weeks.

Victor Murgaski

A Vacation with Pay

In the early years of the war, Victor Murgaski got several deferments from military call-up because of his work in a military vehicle testing program at a Chrysler plant in Windsor, Ontario. He joined up in 1944, was sent overseas about a year later and arrived in England just in time for VE-Day. He was then sent to Belgium where he contracted pneumonia and was consequently classified fit for light duty only.

About six weeks after I arrived overseas the army decided to send me to the Netherlands as a physical education instructor. I had been the captain of my soccer team at school and was quite athletically inclined, but I didn't really know anything about athletic training. I was sent to Apeldoorn where the troops were given the opportunity to prepare for Allied athletic meets. When I got there the soldiers were getting ready for some sort of military olympics that was to take place in Berlin, and I was asked to train the Canadian army sprinters. The facilities at Apeldoorn were excellent; they included not only a good running track—and a sizable number of Canadian soldiers wanted to run—but also there was a stable with some beautiful horses in it. So I got onto a horse and rode around while training the volunteers for the sprinting competition. Well, there was a fellow standing on the side, a Dutchman, who was watching all of this, and he said to me, "Hey, I guess you don't really know what you are doing, do you?" So I asked him if he did. It turned out that he had a master's degree in physical education from the University of Amsterdam, and I asked him if he wanted to work for the

Victor Murgaski in the Netherlands.

Canadian army. Well, he cost me two or three hundred cigarettes a month, plus some food, and from then on I exercised the horses while he exercised the sprinters. He did such a wonderful job that it wasn't long before the army realized that I wasn't doing very much; so they sent me to Amsterdam for a few weeks and then on to Nijmegen where I helped to train people in a boxing school.

After a short period of work in Germany at a technical school, I went back to Amsterdam and was posted to a Canadian army leave

At the boxing school at Nijmegen.

157

centre. I was made the assistant to a fellow from the YMCA who was in charge of the leave centre's canteen. When soldiers would arrive on leave from Germany or other parts of the Netherlands, they would sleep in this building and we provided them with everything they needed. I actually was billeted in a warehouse that was full of chocolates and cigarettes. This was a damn hazardous position, and I even carried a gun. In fact I would guard the stores as well as distribute them. At the warehouse one night there was an incident: I woke up and heard noises of people crawling up the side of the building to my room on the second floor, so I took my gun and sprayed the windows with shot. When I got to the windows and looked down, I could see three guys hightailing it; they were wearing the square caps which were part of the uniforms of Dutch policemen.

Anything that soldiers prized or wanted was in that warehouse. One of the reasons I think I got the position was that I myself didn't smoke or drink, and I was also in good physical condition. Sometimes I was authorized to dispose of large quantities of goods in order to obtain money for compassionate purposes. This could have been dangerous—the black marketeers knew who in the Canadian army was carrying money. When I went out I carried a revolver in my tunic for self-protection. Some soldiers who drank too much would end up in a canal. You'd be walking along and anyone could just shove you in and grab your kit bag with all your belongings. There were desperate people, some of whom had been sympathetic to the other side, who didn't know how they were going to make out after the war and turned to crime. Canadians were warned to stay out of certain areas and specific establishments.

I had a lot of money. I could have taken anything I wanted from the warehouse, but I didn't have to because I got my own issue of cigarettes and I didn't smoke. There were thousands of soldiers going home every month and the cigarettes that were sent to them kept arriving. If a soldier came in and asked me for a hundred cigarettes, he would think I was being generous when I gave him five times that amount, but I was sitting on a quantity of fifty thousand. If a guy came in and said he had been rolled, you'd replace everything he had had with him and then some. The idea was that these troops were in Amsterdam on leave and were supposed to have a nice time. Of course, there were some guys who couldn't control themselves; they would get drunk, pay outrageous prices for a dance and do other things like that.

After the war the Netherlands economy was stagnant. The Canadian troops really helped to stabilize things. We brought in food, equipment, gasoline and oil, parts, tools, and a lot of this material went to the Dutch. In addition, we employed Dutch personnel at the service establishments set up for the soldiers. The Canadians were certainly no detriment to the Dutch economy. Much of our equipment stayed in the Netherlands. When I left, I personally had to turn over the car I was driving to a Dutch government minister.

And what did the Canadians take for their cigarettes? Maybe a dance, a couple of good

With two friends in Amsterdam.

nights out, some black-market booze, some damn good meals. You could buy barbequed chicken on the beach on Scheveningen; it was expensive, but the Canadians had the money to buy it. That meant some Dutchmen were raising and selling those chickens and getting paid for it.

When I was working at the leave centre I decided that I needed to be mobile, so I requisitioned a vehicle. I wanted to go high class, so instead of having an army vehicle issued to me, I requisitioned, from collaborators' property that had been seized, a 1941 Buick and had it painted army green. This car was very popular. When senior army officers saw the vehicle they would ask me to join them and take them for a ride. The car had all the proper army labels and a little union jack that I flew in front on special occasions.

The officers decided that this car was exactly what they needed so they assigned the car, and me with it as driver, to Headquarters Inquiries Section. This section was responsible for bringing to trial Canadians who had committed crimes in the Netherlands. Usually I would drive the officers to the hearings in the mornings and pick them up in the afternoons. During the days I could listen to the proceedings and often I was free to do anything else I pleased.

One day when I knew I wouldn't be needed, I asked the officer in charge for permission to go to the airport. I wanted to see Winston Churchill who was arriving for a visit. The officer said okay and told me not to get into any trouble. I sat in the back seat of the car dressed in a leather jerkin and balmoral, a friend of mine drove, and we flew the union jack, which normally indicated that a senior official was being chauffeured around. We drove right down the main street where the throngs were lining the sidewalks waiting for Churchill; they waved to me and I waved back. Then, with our union jack flying, we drove straight into the airport, unchallenged, past the guard of honour. Churchill was just arriving, and I got out of the car and proceeded to take photographs until some Dutch colonel figured out that this was a ruse. The guy grabbed me and we began to wrestle right on the tarmac while the ceremonies were still going on. Well, they broke us apart, and later the newspapers reported that a Dutch colonel had ejected an unruly Canadian.

In due time I was paraded in front of the commanding officer. He told me that he had heard about a fracas at the airport; I agreed that I had also heard about it and said I sympathized with the Canadian involved and respected his desire not to be pushed around. The commanding officer was waiting for me

The driver beside his car.

to admit that I was the one involved, but he would not ask the question directly. So I said: "Sir, all I can tell you is that the Canadian gave a darn good account of himself," and the officer said that was all he wanted to hear, and that was the end of the hearing.

There was a lot of crime, mostly petty, but little of it was detected. Most of it involved theft: a brigadier was court-martialed when a few train loads of supplies for which he was responsible disappeared; a truckload of booze was stolen; a sergeant-major on inspection parade was told to roll up his sleeves and was found to have gold watches all the way up both arms—those were some of the things that happened. There were also some incidents involving Canadian soldiers and former

Photographing Churchill.

members of the Dutch underground. Some of the girls that soldiers dated had been "collaborators"—they had previously gone with German soldiers. The Canadians couldn't care less, and when the underground went after those girls, the soldiers became their protectors and got into trouble.

One of the last things I did, after the court-martial hearings were over, was to pick up war brides in my car and transport them to headquarters prior to their departure to Canada. If they needed them, the brides could get extra clothes from the Red Cross. They could also exchange their guilders—actually their dowries—for Canadian money up to a limit of fifteen hundred dollars per war bride. Now a lot of them didn't have very much money. I would ask them what they had and if it wasn't enough, I would provide them with the rest of the guilders they needed. This was another one of the benefits from the sale of surplus cigarettes. Some of the girls were marrying Canadians who had virtually nothing. I knew that, but they didn't. What if the girl didn't like Canada? How would she get back home? That's why I helped out. Of course, this wasn't done officially, but some of the officers knew about it and there was tacit approval.

The Canadians were well looked after in the Netherlands. They were in good physical condition, had a lot of money and were attractive to women. Some Dutchmen thought the Germans had been better gentlemen and perhaps they had good reason to say so. After the war in Holland they used to sing this song:

When the *Canadees* comes to Amsterdam
All the *Hollandse Meisjes* [girls] feel very glad;
Rook de peukie [smoke the butt], eat *chocoladen*,
Make *Canadees* very hot.

This was the image of the Canadian.

The sad part concerned the CWAC [Canadian Women's Army Corps] women who got overseas; no one would go after them. They were usually older and hard to get along with because of the Victorian type of training they had received back home. The nurses were the same—if you went out with them it was almost an act of social kindness. They would

Murgaski takes a Dutch bride.

(Opposite) Victor Murgaski today is Humanities Master at Centennial College in Scarborough, Ontario.

go to the dances, but the important point was who you went home with. In many instances, the Dutch girls virtually threw themselves at our soldiers. Many Dutchmen were very tough and expected a lot from their women; in contrast, the Canadian soldiers treated Dutch women like a million dollars. Another factor was the population balance: in Canada there were equal numbers of males and females, but in the Netherlands the Dutch boys had been sent to the colonies, or to the armed forces, or to labour camps during the war, and after there were many more women available.

(Below) On the Dutch-German border.

DAVID KAUFMAN

In 1946 I attended a farewell party. In a skit all the different troops were depicted: they showed the American with his sloppy salute, the German goose-stepping, and the little Englishman saluting the corporal and hopping around like a jaybird. And then, all of a sudden, the whole house came down. Here comes the Canadian: one girl on each arm, a carton of cigarettes and a bottle of whiskey in his hands, drunk as can be. People laughed and cheered. But I also saw another farewell, in Oldenburg, Germany. When the Canadians were pulling out, the women and children were waving, but they looked rather sad. Then I found out what was happening: right behind the Canadians, in were marching the Poles. Even in Germany the Canadians had treated people in a friendly way.

Herbert Frederick Feaver

Give and Take

Herbert Frederick Brooks-Hill "Temp" Feaver spent six months during the early part of the war in Tokyo as a diplomatic hostage of the Japanese. He returned to Canada safely and in March 1945 was appointed first secretary to the Canadian legation serving Allied governments located in London during the hostilities.

I go back to Holland once in a while for a visit and I still have some sort of kindred feeling towards the Dutch. The whole thing was a kind of wonderful experience I can reflect back on—like a dream. I often think of it as a kind of vacation with pay; after all, I didn't kill anyone and I had a wonderful time.

I also think, that when all is said and done, the Canadians were so friendly towards the Dutch that they were thought of as pure, naive people who had gone to the Netherlands out of a sense of adventure. When the Canadians had been in France it was wartime, and everyone was preoccupied with survival; in Belgium, half the population had been sympathetic to the Germans; but in the Netherlands the Dutch saw us liberate their country and saw our soldiers give up their lives. All during the war, the Dutch had despised the Germans who mistreated them. The Canadians were the first friendly people on the scene, the first people to show respect and warmth. The paradox, when you consider the long history of Dutch exploration and colonization, is that it was a primitive, new country like Canada that was willing to go in and do the job of rescue. The Dutch knew that Canada had not hand-picked the Netherlands, but they liked Canadians.

Several days after the surrender of the Germans in northwest Europe, I was flown into the Netherlands by a special aircraft of the RCAF. To start with, I went to see General Foulkes at Hilversum. I actually arrived on a tandem bicycle and left in a limousine which was lent to me by the General and which he, in turn, had obtained from a Dutch businessman who had hidden it during the war. There was still no coal or electricity or transport, and I could only move about under army auspices and live and eat in the army mess. As a civilian, I was much less conspicuous than Canadians in army uniform. When they were recognized you saw a general demonstration of goodwill extended to them by the Dutch people; but I had no Canadian label on me and was usually an observer of these demonstrations of friendship.

My job was to help plan for the re-opening of the Canadian legation in The Hague. I had to assist in finding suitable quarters and trying to make contact with the staff that had worked in the legation before the war. This was a gradual process, and while we were locating the building for the residence and the chancery, we operated out of a hotel. The furniture that had been in what was eventually our legation residence had been seized by a German general who had occupied the building during the war. I made a trip through devastated Germany to try to find the furniture, but when I got to the place where the objects were reputed to be stored, they had disappeared.

Our relations with Canadian military were very good throughout, but it was only with the gradual withdrawal of Allied forces that we began to assume more and more of the daily contacts between our government and that of the Netherlands. At an early stage we dealt with Dutch war brides who wanted to go to Canada. Later on we dealt more with immigrants. As a result of the war, the Dutch East Indies became the independent nation of Indonesia, and the movement of emigrants from the Netherlands to its former colony had stopped. This in turn marked the beginning of a great flood of Dutch people who requested permission to immigrate to Canada.

Prospective immigrants would first be sent to the Dutch Emigration Service where they would be checked for their security records among other things. The Dutch government was not sending its undesirables abroad; they wanted the immigrants to be a credit to their country and a success in Canada. Once they were approved by the Dutch, the prospective immigrants were, more or less, given a rubber stamp of approval by our office, medically examined, then sent on, often on ships that were chartered by the Dutch government itself. In the case of war brides, as far as we were concenred they were already Canadian citizens by virture of their marrying our soldiers, and all we had to do was provide passports. The passage of war brides was considered a military matter.

One of the problems after the war was the disposition of surplus army equipment. Initially there had been a suggestion that the

Herbert Frederick Feaver.

equipment be sold off piece by piece, but that was thought to be unsatisfactory. I finally helped to work out a blanket arrangement with the Dutch foreign minister, who was a personal friend of mine. The Canadian army had taken over many public buildings in the Netherlands for military purposes, so a fair price was established for this accommodation and, in exchange, the Netherlands was offered military equipment at bargain prices. Certain equipment was sent back to Canada but the rest, especially vehicles and machines that had been damaged in the fighting, was turned over to help the Dutch armed forces re-equip themselves. These materials had already been paid for and had served their purposes, and therefore constituted no additional burden on the Canadian taxpayer. At this time of aid to the devastated European countries, we were certainly not trying to do any hard bargaining.

The Wives Bureau

Due to the pressure upon the military to bring Canadian soldiers home, there was initially inadequate attention paid to the transportation and other problems of Dutch women who had married soldiers. This situation is described by an officer who worked in the Dutch Wives Bureau.

One of the serious problems that occurred months after the war was over in the Netherlands was that of taking care of women who had married or become romantically involved with Canadian soldiers. I was marrying a Dutch girl and did not know how I was going to get her back to Canada. Several officers took an interest in these problems and brought them to the attention of the Canadian Ambassador to The Hague, Pierre Dupuy. This resulted in a recommendation to the Canadian government that a Dutch Wives Bureau be set up immediately in our embassy. I became the first officer to serve in the bureau and began my work there in December 1945, just after our honeymoon.

There were a lot of practical problems to be dealt with in transporting Dutch war brides to Canada, one of which was insuring the girls' luggage. Most of the soldiers, upon returning home, had left their wives or fiancées with Dutch guilders and little else except the promise that, somehow, the Canadian army would get them over to Canada. It was terribly important to the women that they be able to insure their luggage and all they had, in most cases, was Dutch currency. I made an appropriate arrangement with the Dutch government, but I was later astounded to find out that the English Wives Bureau, to whom I was ostensibly reporting, had killed the agreement. Instead, we received instructions that the insurance had to be purchased through a major Canadian company and paid for in dollars.

I eventually discovered that the Canadian insurance company specified by the English Wives Bureau had been paying kick-backs to a high ranking officer in that bureau and that the officer simply wanted to extend his money-making program into the Netherlands.

This all blew up when the officer in question came to Holland with his second-in-command and we had a face to face meeting in an office at the embassy. There I was, a junior officer facing a colonel and a major, and I accused them both of taking rebates on luggage insurance policies and committing several other offences.

The result of this was that they placed me under arrest. However, I refused to leave the office and pointed out that, under army regulations, I could only be kept under the guard of another Canadian officer. To my good fortune, they were in a great rush to get back to England, and as there were no other Canadian officers available in The Hague that afternoon, they decided to release me an hour later.

I immediately contacted a friend of mine who was a diplomat in our embassy and, as the result of his advice, I told my story to the ambassador the next morning. A senior Canadian officer posted in England came to take evidence from me, and the colonel was placed under arrest, court-martialled, and dismissed from the army. Ambassador Dupuy also made sure that other irregularities were taken care of and never allowed to get started in the Dutch Wives Bureau.

By this time, women who had married Canadian soldiers or who had become pregnant were beginning to come to the embassy for help. Under Dutch law, women who married Canadians lost their Dutch citizenship, and there were cases in which over-zealous municipal officials had deprived these women of their ration coupons, thus causing the expectant mothers serious nutritional problems. These cases were documented by a newly arrived embassy medical officer whose brother was a prominent Liberal party senator. When we brought these problems to the attention of Dupuy, the ambassador sent a telegram to Prime Minister Mackenzie King saying that he would not continue to be responsible for Canada's relations with the Netherlands if something was not done about the problems immediately.

This combination of lobbyists had the desired effect, and by mid-1946 there were fifteen or twenty officers and two Red Cross nurses working full-time in the Wives Bureau at the embassy, and women were finally being sent over to Canada. I have no doubt that as there were more than a hundred thousand soldiers to repatriate, the plight of their wives seemed less urgent; after all, there were many mothers who wanted their sons back home. But once the problems with the English Wives Bureau were cleared up, things proceeded in a much smoother way in the Netherlands.

Norman Penner

As Others Saw Us

DAVID KAUFMAN

Norman Penner, a professor of political science at York University, served with the Royal Canadian Corps of Signals in a unit attached to the British 107th Brigade.

When the war ended in the Netherlands, we were at a military camp in Oldenzaal, near the German border. We were summoned by our major to hear an important statement, which he then read to us, saying that the war had ended. Of course we were extremely happy and went on a few binges, but that was about all. We weren't near any large population centre where we could share in the celebrations. I had dinner that night in Oldenzaal with a family that I had befriended. Their son had been a Dutch underground fighter and had been killed. They had his picture draped in black on their wall and were very sad that he had died before the war ended. These and other Dutch people were extremely friendly to us. It was a good feeling.

We had been in Germany and had seen the slave labour camps, the German farms well stocked with animals, the German homes with goods brought back from the surrounding countries. In France, Belgium, and the Netherlands everything was denuded—the people were impoverished. And yet the people of these three countries were very hospitable, even though they had been robbed by the Germans and remained with virtually nothing.

The feeling that you were really welcome in the Netherlands had a tremendous impact on the Canadian army. In our minds, there was no doubt that we had been fighting a just war, but the understanding that we also had been fighting on *behalf* of these people reinforced our conception of the war. It was a feeling of solidarity as well as friendship. This was a lasting memory that all Canadians took home with them.

The other positive aspect of our presence on the continent was that we were recognized by others as Canadians and we recognized ourselves as Canadians. This hadn't been the case back home. When I had joined the army, I was asked for my nationality and when I said Canadian, the army wouldn't accept that. In Winnipeg in 1941 you were not recognized as a Canadian, but were identified by what your father was, or grandfather or great-grandfather. There was no legal definition of a Canadian. But when we went overseas, for the first time in our lives we felt that we represented Canada. In Europe the badge on our shoulder meant something.

The nationalism of these Canadian boys was a direct result of their participation in the war. It was a good kind of nationalism—not accompanied by a sense of superiority at all. It became widely recognized that we had taken our place among the soldiers of other nations and had helped to win this great world struggle.

(Opposite) A funeral procession for forty-five members of the Dutch underground killed by the Germans.

Public Archives Canada, DND 54102 / M.M. Dean

A funeral service for Canadian soldiers who had not been properly buried before.

The citizens of Wierden unveil a plaque commemorating the liberation of their town by the Algonquin Regiment.

Public Archives Canada, DND 55403 / B.J. Gloster

166

Public Archives Canada, DND 55958 / C.H. Richer

In a ceremony on July 20, 1945, General Crerar was invested as a Knight of the Grand Cross of the Order of Orange Nassau by Prince Bernhard.

(Overleaf) The farewell parade of the Royal Winnipeg Rifles at Ede on November 7, 1945.

Public Archives Canada. DND 58533 / Ken Bell.

Dutch children watch a farewell parade.

Public Archives Canada, DND 58779 / Ken Bell

Epilogue

By mid-winter of 1946 the remaining Canadian uniforms in the Netherlands were rare. Dutch society was slowly returning to normal, or what passed for it in those days; full economic recovery was still years away. Meanwhile large numbers of Canadian servicemen were returning to a country that was resolutely set on a course towards economic expansion.

In the late war years the prospect of reconstruction had been much in the minds of Canadians. Politicians and civil servants worried about a return of the depressed conditions of the 1930s; they were not alone. Indeed, the democratic socialist movement which had taken shape in the early Depression years, the Cooperative Commonwealth Federation, gained considerable support after 1941 because a growing number of Canadians believed neither of the two major parties could be trusted to win the peace. And what was the point of winning the war if a new depression should follow? In some circles too there were fears of the sort of unrest that had accompanied the end of the first World War.

Faced with a threat from its political left, the federal Liberal government led by William Lyon Mackenzie King committed itself in 1944-45 to a program of improved social security measures and of economic growth. It also took steps to ensure the war veterans were integrated into civilian life more smoothly than had been the case a quarter century earlier. Many of them went back to school at public expense; for several years universities were crowded with men many of whom might otherwise have never had this opportunity.

Economic expansion is in Canadian minds inextricably linked to large-scale immigration. During the bleak 1930s there had been little; in the war it had been impossible to import manpower, particularly after the United States entered the war. As a consequence, women had entered the labour force as never before, encouraged by unprecedented provisions for child care.

These did not long survive the war. In order to free up jobs in the manufacturing and service sectors for returning soldiers, married women were encouraged to get back into the kitchens and nurseries. But there were continuing shortages of labour in some areas. Industrialization and urbanization, both of which had accelerated during the war, drew men away from the fields, forests and mines. These offered occupations that were regarded, not without reason, as dirty, ill-paid, lacking prestige, and that were generally available only in more or less remote places—in a word, unattractive. However, although the government wished to encourage the growth of manufacturing, it recognized that agriculture and the primary, extractive industries would continue to be the backbone of Canadian exports. Furthermore, to the provinces the primary sector represented an important source of government revenue.

The country's industrial policies required immigration. As in the early twentieth century and in the 1920s, immigrants would make up labour shortages in agriculture, mining, and the forest industry, and—an important consideration—could be expected to do so at a relatively low cost. Thus, when an immigration policy was enunciated in

1946-47, it looked specifically to the importation of immigrants who would not stay in the cities but would go where the rough work needed doing.

The Netherlands was an obvious source especially of farmers and farm labourers. As one of its post-war reconstruction policies, the Dutch government was offering inducements to surplus farm workers to emigrate. They pressed too heavily on the land. Here was an opportunity for Canada to secure immigrants who were eager to make a new and presumably better life for themselves, and who were expected to fit easily into the dominant ethnic and social patterns of the country.

Not only did the federal government recruit immigrants; in August 1947 a meeting took place in The Hague between two emissaries of the Ontario government, Thomas Kennedy, the Minister of Agriculture, and Dana Porter, the Minister of Immigration, Planning and Development, and Willem Drees, Dutch Minister of Social Affairs, who was responsible for emigration. According to the representative from the Canadian embassy who kept minutes, the two Ontarians spoke highly of the Dutch immigrants who had settled in Canada in the past. "The Netherlands Minister replied that he was most happy to hear such glowing reports of the achievements of his countrymen in Canada, and in view of the friendly relations established between the Netherlands and Canada by the liberation and by the later residence of troops here, he was certain that very great numbers of Dutch emigrants would wish to go to Canada."

In fact the first group of post-war Dutch immigrants (other than the war brides) had already arrived. The ship *Waterman* docked in Montreal on June 27, 1947 with approximately 1,000 potential farmers, creating, according to one newspaper report, "the busiest steamship passenger disembarkation since pre-war ocean arrival days." A second ship, the *Tabinta*, arrived in Montreal in mid-September. The flood of Dutch immigration had begun. In the quarter century that followed almost 200,000 Netherlanders entered Canada. And while the early immigrants were predominantly farming folk, changes in Canadian immigration policy meant that people from all walks of life came.

After ten years of economic depression—the Low Countries were hard hit by the slump of the 1930s—and five years of war, not a few Netherlanders were bound to look for something better than they were likely to find in their native country. The loss in 1948-49 of the Dutch East Indies, and the realization that Dutch recovery depended in large part on the speed of German recovery, sharpened the sense of inadequate opportunity. Basic to the thoughts of almost all who contemplated emigration in the 1940s and 1950s was the belief that the new world offered more than the old, if not to oneself then to one's children.

Those who actually took the wrenching step most frequently chose Canada. Had the quota system not been in effect in the United States it is conceivable that most emigrants might have gone there instead. Canada was in any case a popular choice. Not only were Netherlanders in obvious demand there, but as a result of the Canadian liberation of the Netherlands most had the feeling that they already knew something about Canada and its people. It was not entirely *terra incognita*, nor was it as far away as Australia, New Zealand or South Africa. Nor was it insignificant that Princess Juliana had spent the war years in Ottawa, and that her third daughter, Margriet, was born there. Canada might be large and cold, but it conjured up a warm and friendly image.

As for the soldiers who fought in the Netherlands and then waited there for repatriation, they have fond memories of the country and its people. Many have gone back over the years to visit, and Canadian tourists generally comment on the warm reception they still get in the Netherlands. Most Canadians are aware of the gifts of tulips with which Queen Juliana annually pays her debt of gratitude to Ottawa and Canada. They also know of the love and respect with which Dutch people tend Canadian war cemeteries. The images again are of warmth and amity.

In the Netherlands as in Canada the legacy of 1944-45 is a somewhat unfocused good feeling. To a majority of those now alive the war is something they hear or read about; so is its aftermath, an irrelevancy, perhaps, in the world of the 1980s. But the older generations still remember. The soldiers and those whom they liberated know what the war was about. They can recall the relief which its end brought, and the thrill of the liberation.

Bibliographical Note

The most important primary source for the historical text was the collection of Army Papers (RG 24) in the Public Archives of Canada, Ottawa. Several Dutch archives also yielded material, as did the invaluable library of the State Institute for War Documentation in Amsterdam.

The most important secondary source was Volume III of the Official History of the Canadian Army in the Second World War, Col. C.P. Stacey's *The Victory Campaign: The Operations in North-West Europe 1944-1945* (Ottawa, 1966). Also very useful were *Out of the Shadows: Canada in the Second World War* (Toronto, 1977) by W.A.B. Douglas and Brereton Greenhous, and *Canada's War: The Politics of the Mackenzie King Government 1939-1945* (Toronto, 1975) by J.L. Granatstein. For the Dutch side, Dr. L. de Jong's magisterial and multivolumed *Het Koninkrijk der Nederlanden in de Tweede Wereldoorlog* (The Hague, 1970ff.) was indispensable. Very serviceable were two books by journalists, Koos Groen's *'Er heerst orde en rust . . .': Chaotisch Nederland tussen September 1944 en December 1945* (Nijmegen & Brugge, 1979) and a lighter-hearted treatment by Michel van der Plas, *Mooie Vrede* (Utrecht, 1966).

Of the numerous regimental and personal accounts three stood out: *Dual Allegiance* (Toronto, 1976) by Ben Dunkelman, *Fun Tomorrow* (Toronto, 1978) by John Morgan Gray, and *The Regiment* (Toronto, 1955) by Farley Mowat. The last of these, a personalized account of the Hastings and Prince Edward Regiment, deals only briefly with the liberation of the Netherlands, but makes for excellent reading.

M.H.

Index

Page numbers in *italic* refer to captions of photographs.